Cast a Long Shadow II

More Reflections on Life

Derek Knight

Foreword

The genesis of this work was a walk along a beach in Norfolk, UK, in the summer of 2011.

It was late afternoon, and I had been thinking for a while about daily writing, and how it would be good to have a prompt to start the process.

I was excited by the prospect of writing, and as I walked with the sun behind me, I saw my shadow stretching out on the path ahead of me. Suddenly I had the title and the theme – a long shadow, and the journey through life.

I first started a blog, and kept it going for 90 days of daily thoughts, which were later published in an edited form as "Cast A Long Shadow – A Reflective Life".

This volume is a fresh collection of these daily thoughts, continuing the journey that we call life.

Derek Knight

March, 2013

Prologue

We all need time to pause and reflect – to take time out of our schedule to be still.

One way of doing this is to consider a word to meditate on – to let our thoughts wonder, and follow them to see where they lead.

This is a collection of 90 "thoughts" prompted by a single word – each word can mean many things to many people, but I hope there may be something here that will help you, Dear Reader, to pause and consider – spending time getting to know yourself a bit better each day as you walk the path of your life.

Unable

A while ago, I had a task to do around the house. At first, I thought it sounded quite complicated, and I just couldn't see how I would be able to do it.

Then I did some investigation, and watched some instructional videos, and soon realized that I could do this after all. But then I started on the first part of the task – and I could not get the very first thing done, so I became discouraged and felt that I was unable to do this straightforward task.

After a while, and with the help of a friend, I tried again, and this time was able to get going, and completed the project with no real problems.

I'm sure we have all had similar experiences, and this points to an interesting facet of human nature – what we are able to do, and what we are not.

Because being "unable" is not necessarily the final answer.

Right now, I am unable to run a marathon. Frankly, I have a hard time imagining me ever doing so. But I also know that, given the right motivation and enough time effort and training I probably could do so. The "unable" here is a reflection of where I am now, and of what I know now.

So much of life is like that. We may be unable to get a better job; unable to change a destructive habit; unable to leave a situation we know to be harmful to us.

But all these things are constrained by what we know now – by our experiences up to date. Some things we may be literally unable to do, but for most things where we use this word, we actually mean that we just can't see a way from here to there; can't see a way out or a way through.

And yet – are these things really impossible, or are we just not yet able to see how to do them?

Like my home improvement project, it may be that we need a little help to start us off, and we can win through. If we are struggling with a bad habit, it may be that we need to admit how much it is actually hurting us before we can move on to the solution.

Whenever we come to a point in our lives where we feel we are unable to take the next step, we need to consider if we are genuinely unable, or just unwilling to change.

Even where we might genuinely want the change, it can seem that we will have to lose so much to get the prize, and so we are unwilling to try for our goal.

But being unable to do something right now can be the springboard to a greater willingness to try. And when we try, there is always hope of success.

Care

I think all of us have a need to feel that someone cares.

No matter how much we may put on a brave face, no matter how much we may say, and even think that we are independent, at heart we respond with gladness when someone cares for us.

And no matter how much of an isolationist we are, there is always something in us that has a need to care for others.

And this caring need not be a physical thing – just to know that someone cares if we are alive that they care enough to check on our well-being, is enough to move us.

This mutual caring is a particularly precious thing, even though sometimes we treat it with little respect. We can sometimes seem to be working against those who care for us, or take little regard of those for whom we should care.

And yet for some of us there are times when we are truly alone, with no one to care for us, and no one to care for.

This may be through our own fault, through circumstance – the reasons are unimportant. What matters is what we do about it.

Do we hide away from all contact, telling ourselves that nobody cares and refusing to help others?

Do we build up resentments against all those who have others to help them, and in this way make ourselves more miserable?

In other words, do we take this lack of care, and build it into something to be miserable about – something that we can fret over and pick at like a sore on our arm?

We don't have to live like that.

Since all of us need to care for someone, and be cared for by someone, we can let that someone be ourselves. We can look after ourselves as we would do a sick friend.

We can see that, even though no one else is there, we can still be caring of the one person that needs care the most – ourselves.

Rather than sitting at home waiting for something to happen, we can go out for a walk and see the world. We can care for our bodily health as we would look after someone recovering from an illness. We can build up our mind and our spirit by caring for them, and not letting our minds fall into disuse, or our spirits diminish.

It may be that, through this self-care, we become people others wish to care for, or that we find others that need our care; but that is not the point of doing it.

The point of self-care is that we need to do it for ourselves, to be true to the God-given creation that is uniquely us.

Scale

Without knowing the scale of something, we can get confused about what is important.

It is like looking at a photograph – is this a picture of a range of mountain from above, or an extreme close up of a grain of sand? Is this a mighty waterfall, or a small stream from a watering can?

When we look closely at a single flower petal, we can be in wonder at the miracle of its construction and its delicate feel. And when we stand back and admire the whole field of flowers, we can feel a totally different wonder at the scale of the beauty and can be captivated by the sight of them all moving in the breeze.

Neither view is "right" nor "wrong" - they are both valid observations, and are different just because of the scale that we are looking at.

When we concentrate only the small-scale, we see just that – the tiny things that happen in our lives. These can be wonderful or not, appealing or not. We can take deep joy from the everyday "little" events in our lives – the simple pleasure of an early morning sunrise, or a late evening stroll.

We can find pleasure in the smallness and closeness of our world, by the feel of a comfortable chair, or the smile of a loved one.

And it is possible to live happily on that scale all of our lives – many people do.

But there is also a larger scale world that we can inhabit. Without losing the joy and contentment of the small-scale, we can also live in a much bigger universe.

This is what I like to call the world of the spirit – the world where we are not just small insignificant beings crawling along on the earth, but we are also players in a much bigger universe.

Here, we can still find our joy in the physical, but also seek a higher calling, a joy on a totally different scale.

For this world is not just the physical, not just the every day. For every flower petal, there is a field of flowers at a greater scale than the petal alone could imagine.

But the field is still composed of individual petals, each unique in its own way.

In the same way, we can live in both scales; in our small physical world, and also in the larger world of the spirit.

There is a joy in both, and in both we can find contentment.

Ground

The ground blow us is supposed to be stable. It is one thing we can count on to stay the same all the time, so much so that we hardly even think about it.

And so when the ground shifts, for example, in an earthquake or a landslide, the shock and fear caused is especially great.

Not only do we have the actual physical problem, but our minds react against the notion that this could happen at all.

Our feelings about the way the world works are shifted and it can take time for us to trust the ground again.

Our understanding has been changed and, instead of a careless assumption that the ground will be solid and unmoving, we are fearful of the ground and subconsciously wonder if it will happen again, and when.

In a similar way, the "solid ground" that are our deeply help beliefs and understanding of life can be challenged.

Someone may have a solid religious belief, but the unexpected death of a loved one can rock the foundation of that belief.

Or another may have a total confidence in the ability of science to answer all possible questions, and then have a sudden spiritual experience that goes beyond their understanding.

When one of these types of experiences happens, and the ground seems to shake beneath our feet, this is indeed a frightening experience. But it can also be an occasion for growth.

Just as a landslide shows us that we have maybe built our house in a bad place, so an emotional landslide can show us that we need to do some more work on our emotional health.

In the same way that an earthquake is destructive to our man-made structures, so a slip in our spiritual ground can be painful and hurt our mental structures.

It can also be an opportunity to rebuild our mental and spiritual foundations on more solid ground.

From time to time, we will all find that what we thought was the solid ground of our beliefs are challenged, and we feel the upset and hurt that comes from that.

But out of the destruction caused, we have the opportunity to rise again, stronger and more fully grounded in the truth.

Hostility

Much as we would like life to go smoothly, we sometimes find hostility in our daily lives.

It may be our fellow workers, family members, business associates, or even strangers in the street, but whatever the source of the hostility, it can affect us in extremely negative ways.

We can strike back in anger; meet hostility with even more hostility. This can soon escalate into a full-on fight, and even draw in others around us. The result can be a long running feud with unpleasant feelings increasing on all sides.

On the other hand, we may not obviously retaliate, but hold the feelings in close to our heart. Thus, it may seem to the outside world that nothing has affected us, until the time when the pressure of holding that anger in is such that it explodes. And then it can appear as if we are the hostile ones because it is not obvious to others where the anger is coming from.

Then again, we may feel such fear that we run and hide; either literally or, more often, figuratively.

This hiding can often take the form of retreating into one self; distancing us from possible harm by not letting anyone close.

This can indeed "protect" us from bad feelings, but it also shields us from any good feelings and positive emotional contact.

In the end, we become disillusioned and depressed because all around us there is only the hostility of others.

Is there no good way to deal with the hostility of others? Must the bully always win?

The fact is we cannot directly change how others react to us – and whilst we can change our behaviors hoping we may influence how others act, there is no guarantee that they will change.

Our best solution in any such situation, is to look to our own actions, and wish the other person well.

That may sound strange – but since we cannot change the other person, the best we can do is to pray that they find happiness, or whatever else it is that they seek, and then look at what we can do.

This does not mean that we have to "put up with" other people's shoddy treatment of us – one of the things we may be able to change is where we are and what we say.

We may be able to speak out own truth quietly, but if not, then we can leave the situation with as much dignity as we are able.

To fight hostility with hostility leads to greater and greater harm. To meet it with love turns the harm aside and allows us to live free.

Greed

All of us want the best – the best for ourselves and for our families, for our loved ones, even for our friends and our acquaintances.

There is nothing wrong with wanting the best; it can be a loving and caring thing.

When we seek to look after our bodies in the right way, when we look to help others to have the best of everything possible, then that is a worthy way to live our lives.

But sometimes we humans can take that wholly good desire, and turn it sour by overuse, because then it becomes greed.

Take the example of food – to look after ourselves properly, we need to eat well and nutritiously. If we skimp on the good things that our bodies need, we will become ill and not able to serve others.

But when that natural desire turns to greed, we are in danger of excess, which causes us not to be healthier, but to become prone to more physical ailments.

Or money – here again, we need some resources to live in this world. None of us can live on air, and we all need some shelter. There may be a few people who can survive on what they can grow and produce themselves, but most of us rely on the concept of money in order to meet our basic physical needs.

It is not money itself that is the root of all evil, but the desire for it. When our natural need to look after ourselves turns to greed, we seek only to make money. We look at the world, not as a wonderful place to live, but as a way of making money. We look at people, not as fellow humans on a journey through life, but as resources to be used in our pursuit of wealth.

When we do this, we succeed only in diminishing ourselves. Whilst we may be rich in terms of cash, we will be poor in terms of spirit and love.

When we are greedy for something, that thing becomes our sole focus, our sole reason for being.

It is this central fact that makes greed such a corrosive force in our lives.

Because when we pursue one thing at the cost of everything else, we lose sight of the central importance of balance in our lives. We make the object of our greed our God, and we daily pray at its altar.

This is why greed becomes unhelpful because although we may "pray" to it, it is a hollow God.

Despite the love we give the object of our greed, it will never love us back.

Fresh

There is something remarkable about mornings, and the freshness of a new day.

Sometimes, I have got up extremely early and been out in the morning seemingly before the rest of the human world is awake.

At those times, the world seems remarkably fresh and clean, and as if the whole of creation is holding its breath, waiting for the day to begin.

And then, there are the "normal" days.

Days when I get up and there are just the tasks that need to be done and projects that need to be completed. The routine, with nothing new or original.

I am sure we have all felt like that from time to time – the feeling of routine, where nothing fresh seems to be likely or even possible.

It is true that we all need to do routine tasks, that we all have things to do that may be repetitive, or that seem pointless. The factory line keeps moving; the office memos keep coming in; the housework seems never to end.

But even in these times, I think it's critical to try to find at least a little that is fresh in every day.

It is beneficial because it is in finding the new and the exciting that we learn more about how to live our lives in a happy and fruitful way.

Even if we have to stack these shelves with the same products that we have every morning for the last 6 years, it can be a fresh experience every day if we challenge ourselves to do it quicker this time, or to strive for perfection in the display.

Even though housework keeps coming, day after day, we can keep it fresh by experience the deep joy of a clean room, or the satisfaction of keeping our surroundings safe for others.

It is not just when we notice freshness that we can experience it – sometimes we have to remind ourselves of the blessing we have, and actively look for the freshness around us.

Although it comes naturally for me to feel the freshness of each day when I get out of the house in the early morning, it can still be a fresh day even if I stay locked in my room writing.

Not only is each day a fresh start – every moment gives us the opportunity for a new beginning.

Don't wait for the perfect day to make a fresh start; start afresh now to make it the perfect day.

Gone

The past has gone; it cannot be brought back.

All our successes in the past have gone.

The competition we won is now just a trophy in the cupboard gathering dust; the firm we started from scratch is now running itself without our help; the work we took such pride in has now been made obsolete by new technology.

All our failures are gone too.

That crucial decision we made that went wrong is now just a memory; the money we spent on a project that ended in failure has gone and been replaced; the relationship we didn't value until it was lost made us different in new relationships.

Can we take nothing from the past – is it all gone?

I think that depends on our understanding; on how we treat that which is gone.

If we try to count yesterday's success as today's victory, we will be disappointed because that success has been done, and cannot be used again.

If we see yesterday's failures as defining us as failures, if we think that we can never succeed because of a failure in the past, we fail to realize that change is possible.

Because although the past is indeed gone, we can take valuable lessons with us into today.

We can – we should – look at both our successes and failures as opportunities for growth.

We can see what worked in the past and rather than trying to replicate it – which would be to try to hold on to what has gone – we can learn about the strengths that helped us.

We can look at our past failures, and rather than dwell on what we did wrong, or how others wronged us, we can look at our shortcomings, and try to learn a better way for the future.

The past has gone and cannot be re-lived.

But the present can be understood with the knowledge of the past, and thus we can make a better future.

Quality

Sometimes, you can meet someone and "just know" that they are trustworthy or not, are friendly or not, are careful or not.

We may or may not be right about these "first impressions", but what is fascinating is that we have them at all.

What it is about these people that makes us think that way?

There seems to be some sort of quality about people that we instinctively connect to.

Some of us are better at picking up on these signals than others; some people get the messages hopelessly wrong, whilst others seem to have an almost physic ability to recognize the quality of others.

But what is it that we see, hear, or even smell that informs this quality judgment?

Much of it could be our experience.

All of us hold in our heads a picture of the universe made up from our previous experiences and interactions.

If we have known people with the same general characteristics as this new person, and our experience has always been that they act in a certain way, our thought will be that this one will be the same.

Much of it may well be assumption.

We may have been taught, for example, that all people like this are not to be trusted, and so the feeling is strong that we will not trust them.

And there will probably be cultural indications too.

There are strong social pressures to like people who are like us, to find some people "attractive" and some not, and to react against things that are not "the norm".

But over and above all these reasons that could be itemized and written down, there also seems to be something else going on.

Sometimes, the quality we find in others cannot be defined in so simplistic a way – it goes beyond reason or prejudice, to something more fundamental and basic.

When we see that quality in someone we truly do "just know" it.

We fall instantly in love with someone. Or we take a dislike so strong that no amount of reason can talk us out of it.

That quality we feel in someone else is beyond mere words, or just thoughts. It touches something deep within our souls.

Force

Sometimes, we are truly forced to do something against our will.

Most of the time, however, we use that expression to mean something we may not want to do, but do because the consequence of not doing it are worse.

Even where there is a law telling us to do something, we are not forced to comply, although if we fail to do so, we know that there will be consequences that we want to avoid.

The fact that there are people who break the law shows us that no one is forced to act in the right way.

That doesn't mean that we shouldn't obey the law, but the act of doing so is not forced on us – it is a choice we make ourselves.

And – for most people – we see the sense in the rule, it accords with our own sense of right and wrong, and we choose to follow it for the good of everyone, including ourselves.

Often, however, we feel that we have no choice – that we are forced to follow a course of action that we do not want to take.

Typically this is not a question covered by laws or rules, but matters of our own conduct.

We may, for example, continue to work at a job because of the force of economic necessity. Or we may be continuing to drink heavily, even when we see how it is damaging us because we feel forced to go to the bar every evening.

In these cases, we need to ask ourselves if we are truly forced to do these things, or if we can change anything.

It may be that we are in debt, or in need of an income to meet our mortgage – but can we find another job, or can we change our outgoings?

It may be that we are feeling compelled to drink every night, but can we seek help with our issues, or change the places we go to?

Humans are free entities, and only in a few cases is there just one course of action, we are not forced to live the way we do.

Sometimes we need to remember that we are free, and act as if we were not forced.

Conceals

Not everything is obvious.

Sometimes, even what seems the most obvious of truths turns out to be at best only partially correct, and sometimes to be woefully inaccurate.

This is because what is obvious often conceals what is true.

To us, it may appear that a friend of ours has it all and is perfectly happy.

They will tell us how fabulous their life is, and even when things seem to be going wrong, somehow they end up being content with their life.

And yet underneath, there is a concealed hurt and frustration that is never given voice.

There can be a deep hurt below the surface that is so well hidden that even they may not recognize it.

In our lives, we need to maintain a balance between concealment and openness.

On the one extreme to be fully revealing to everyone opens us up for hurt and can put too large a burden on others – it can be a way of dumping our hurt on other people, just to make us feel good.

To spend 30 minutes telling the store clerk all my troubles may make me feel that I am being open – in fact, I am just venting to no good purpose. Not everybody need to know the minutia of my life, and to try to impose that burden on them is to make small Gods of the people I meet.

But at the other end of the scale, to conceal all my troubles, even from my closest friend or partner, is harmful to both them and us, as there is nothing that promotes closeness so much as shared sorry or happiness.

If I am suffering in silence, and not letting anyone in, I am showing that I do not feel they are good enough to help, or maybe that I feel uniquely awful and uniquely unable to be helped.

Strange as it may seem, this is a manifestation of pride, of believing myself to be different, rather than just another human being, doing the best they can.

The balance here is in knowing what should be concealed, and from whom.

Or, to put it another way, to know whom to be fully frank and open with.

Because there are those occasions and those people with whom we should be open, and there are those things that need to be concealed from most people.

Sometimes we will get this wrong, and reveal too much to someone who proves to be untrustworthy, or conceal something from someone we should have confided in.

But learning the balance is just part of our journey through life.

Soul

Is this all there is?

Is the only point in life to make as much money as possible? Is it true "life's a bitch, and then you die"?

Some would tell us that this is the case – that we are just machines, which react as we are programmed to react.

And yet such an explanation is unsatisfactory because it ignores our human condition.

I am not saying that religious organizations have a complete answer to everything, nor that science cannot teach us anything; the truth is not that simple.

Religion once told us that the world was flat, that slavery was an acceptable form of business and that women should not vote.

Science produces theory after theory on how things work, each one promoted as the truth until another theory comes along.

And so if one party tells us that we have a soul, and the other that we do not, who are we to believe?

I think the answer is to trust ourselves, and try to keep away from assumptions.

Because what does it actually mean, to have a soul?

For me, it is a word I use to express the essence of a person, which is distinct from, but connected to their body.

When a close friend dies, even the most hardened of atheists will often say that the person is "looking down on them" that something about them is still here.

There is the deep human feeling that we are not alone, that some essence of the person is still with us.

For many of us, the questions of what or how are irrelevant because we know, deep inside us that there is something more than just the physical.

I have experienced this, and yet I know that the experience was personal to me, I cannot convince a doubter of how it felt or what I now feel.

And nor do I need to – we all have our own path to walk, and no one has a monopoly on truth.

For now, it is enough to know our own truth, and continue the journey.

Valuable

What we consider of value will be different from what other people do. Even in our own lives, our value system can change over time.

Many of us are brought up believing that getting a good education is all important, and indeed that can be a valuable asset in our career.

The modern world encourages us to place value on money and worldly riches. Our media encourage us to live the "good life" that only money can buy – it tells us that we will be happy if we get this car, or that piece of electronics; that if we owned the billion dollar home we would then undoubtedly have made it.

There is no particular virtue in being poor, because money does make life easier in a lot of ways.

But are these truly the most valuable things in our lives?

For all our education, things change and new knowledge is gained, making our old learning redundant. If we use our knowledge to make ourselves more fulfilled, then that is to the good, but it is the fulfillment, rather than the knowledge that is valuable.

And whilst money can keep us from being miserable, it cannot make us happy.

Surrounding ourselves with the best of everything will help to make our lives easier, but what will we do with the ease that it provides?

I believe that what is valuable is not easily measured by the outside world.

In terms the world understands, a large mansion with acres of land will be more valuable than a small town-house in a city side street.

But if the town-house is a refuge for a person who is only seeking quiet and peace – to them, it is much more valuable than a mansion.

What is valuable to us is not always easily able to be quantified and measured.

Sometimes there will be an item that brings us inner peace, but mostly the things that make us the happiest are not things.

Who can put a value on a grandchild's smile, or the touch on our hand by a loved one? What is the price of the feeling of awe as we watch the sun set into the evening sky?

Money, possessions – the things we surround ourselves with can be replaced.

It is the intangible things that give us joy and cannot be replaced and that are our most valuable assets.

Repose

In can be difficult in our everyday world to find quiet restfulness, peace and tranquility – to find true repose.

There is so much that demands our attention. There are deadlines to meet, activities to be undertaken, decisions to be made.

With all this activity, how is it possible to find repose? Is it even necessary?

It is possible to carry on each day with activity after activity – with nothing but movement. When we do we find that there are still more demands, still more things that need to be done.

It is possible to live life this way – but it is not desirable, because out of repose comes greater self-awareness and fulfillment.

Even if it seems that nothing constructive was achieved, the act of being in mindful repose is effective in itself.

Stopping from our activities can be hard; it seems like we are a failure if we stop what we are doing, and do nothing.

But in that state of peace of the body, we can find peace of mind. Just as our physical body needs the escape of sleep, so our spirit needs repose to re-charge itself.

The mind is a marvelous thing – it will continue to work away at resolving problems long after they have finished. It also keeps on planning the future and trying to anticipate where we are going.

This happens whether we are conscious of it or not, and often this busyness of our brains can seep over into our physical activities too.

All of this activity is wearing on our spirit, on that part of us which is uniquely us.

We need activity, but we also need peace. We need thought, but we also need inner quiet.

Balance is once again the key here – to take no mental or physical activity is clearly detrimental to us, but so too much.

In our life, we need time for repose for our mind and body. To keep pushing on may seem the best that can be done, but sometimes the best we can do is to rest.

And often, out of that time of quiet repose comes renewed vigor; a new outlook on a problem.

Most importantly, repose can re-energize us in our journey to true contentment.

Wash

All creatures seem to have an instinctive desire to be clean: just look at birds preening, cats grooming – even pigs wallowing in mud are washing themselves in their own way.

For us humans, washing often has social significance, in addition to the practical.

Many cultures practice either actual or symbolic cleaning ceremonies to mark rites of passage.

This idea of washing goes deep into our minds, and it has spread into our language about how society works; we "wash our hands" of a situation, and "make a clean start".

And so the significance of being washed is more to us than just the practical. It is not just our bodies that feel in need of cleaning, but our hearts, minds and spirits.

Just as we could ignore the dirt on our bodies, we are able to ignore the clutter that can inhabit our souls, but to wash them clean is not only a necessity, it is a pleasure.

After a long day of work, it feels pleasurable to wash that dirt away and dress in clean clothes.

In a similar way, a period of quiet contemplation will clear the clutter from our minds, and leave us refreshed and ready to tackle new challenges.

It is often after such quiet times that I am at my most productive, and this seems to be because I have washed away all the old thoughts, and allowed space for the new to come in.

A time of meditation, when we stop our constant rush to achieve can allow our souls to sour, to reach for the stars again.

When I am particularly troubled by something, a period when I do not concentrate on the issue, but instead concern myself with my inner being, washes my tendency to gloom and introspection away.

Instead, I am able to go on with renewed vigor, and face the world afresh.

We wash our hands to try to keep our bodies safe from harm; so should we take care to keep our hearts clean, to save our spirit from the grime of our daily journey through life.

Far

When we are young, it seems that the future is far away and that a trip to the next block is a voyage to a distant land.

As we get older, time seems to speed up, and those places that seemed impossibly far away become extremely close, but even so some places seem exotic and far distant.

And so it seems our perception of what is far away – either in terms of time or physical distance – can change as we experience more and learn more.

For some of us, any experience that is not quantified by length and breadth, by physical laws and explainable truth, is too far from our comprehension to be considered real.

Many of us start off life with some sort of education in religious or anti-religious beliefs, but these are just learned, not what we truly feel.

With increasing experience, a lot of us turn our backs on that learning, and go our own way without regard to anything that we cannot see, hear or touch.

But even then, we often feel that something is missing, something that is elusive and far away, but worth striving for.

Much of human history - good and evil - is about that striving for something far distant. Lands have been settled, wars fought, forms of government created and abandoned in the search for the perfect way to live.

And yet that ideal is still as far away as it was when we started.

There may be times when we think we have found the solution, but ever human endeavor eventually falls into disrepute and disrepair.

Is there no solution then? Is everything futile?

I think that the answer is in the journey.

Human life will never be perfect, but we can strive for perfection none the less. We cannot be happy all the time, but we can seek for happiness. No form of government will ever be ideal in all situations, but we can continue to look for improved ways of organizing our common life.

The future remains far away, and this is something to be celebrated because it gives us a purpose in life; it gives our journey a meaning.

The destination may be too far to reach today, but we can live today going towards that ideal, and we will get there one day at a time.

Bravery

There are many kings of bravery, it is true, but I find myself questioning if some things the world calls brave are actually the ones we should celebrate.

It is not just a question of the fine line between bravery and foolishness, although there is often that too, but what may appear brave to others, is sometimes just what needs to be done.

A while ago I moved to a new town in a new county, where I didn't know anyone or have any connections at all.

Some people thought me foolish, others thought me brave, to do such a thing.

In fact, I do not consider myself to be either – it was the best solution to the situation I was in, and I simply trusted my guiding spirit to lead me where I needed to be.

Once I worked in an office with someone who was blind.

He came to work every day like the rest of us and worked at his desk like everyone else, and some said how brave he was to do so.

However, to him such comments were not welcome – for he was just getting on with his life, the same way everyone else tried to. For him, to say that he was brave for living his life was as demeaning as to it would have been to say that he was not good enough to work in the office because of his blindness.

Bravery cannot truly be judged by looking at the actions people take, but should be looked at by the feelings inside us.

If we take an action without feeling any fear – no matter how "dangerous" it may appear to others – are we truly showing bravery, or are we showing faith?

When I moved towns, I had faith that it was the right thing to do – there was the worry about how to do it, but no worry that doing it was wrong.

My friend in the office had faith in his ability to do the job – he may have been apprehensive when he started about working in a strange environment – but he knew that his ability would see him through.

Faith makes bravery redundant because it means that we can look at the fear, and know that it is groundless.

Building

Different images come to mind with the word "building".

I remember the City I once worked in, a modern financial district where the concrete seemed endless. I think in particular of an open plaza there, surrounded by tall office buildings, where there was, of all things, a skating rink.

This seems the precise essence of buildings – strong and designed for work and play.

But no sooner does my mind think of that type of building, than it turns to another – a lighthouse on a sea facing cliff.

Nothing could be more different or more similar – again there is the man-made structure, but here it is in a wild and open area because the lighthouse I am thinking of is on the coast a long way from any other building.

Whereas the City buildings are the same night or day, rain or shine, the lighthouse can be a welcoming haven from a wild winter storm, or a comforting familiar landmark as one walks along the shore on a summer day.

And that feeling of the familiar brings to mind the many homes I have lived in, for a short or a long time.

My first memories are of a terraced house in a small railway town, soon to be replaced by a seaside house where sea gulls screeched and made their nests in our roof.

I have called home a modern hill top bungalow, an ancient cottage by a river, a large suburban family house, and a tiny one room studio apartment.

All different locations and building styles, yet all places that were once more than a building, they were a home.

And even the term home brings to mind other buildings that were not "home", but were places I stayed and became attached to.

The upmarket Hotel that I stayed in week after week when I was working on a project became a kind of home – a place that I knew so well that it became normal to stay there.

And that, maybe, is why the unadorned word "building" brings so many thoughts.

A building may appear to be only a collection of concrete and brick, but it is a place that holds our memories.

And just as our memories are part of whom we are, so too are all the buildings that we have inhabited, because they still inhabit us.

Alteration

Many things alter in our lives, and there is only one certainty; everything changes.

We can be scared of that alteration in our lives – we are naturally inclined to want to hold things unaltered. However, even when it seems that the current situation is ideal, it is not only futile to hold onto it, but when we try to do so we build up harm for ourselves.

It may be that we have an old destructive habit or addiction, but even knowing that it is destructive, we seem unable to let go of that old way of life, and accept an alteration in our way of thinking.

And yet such an alteration - sometimes a drastic one - is needed if we are ever to be truly free and live the lives that we are intended to.

Or sometimes we find that people we assumed would never change have altered. This can be particularly hard when as an adult child our parents separate, or otherwise change their life-style. It can be easy to say "but what about me? Did you consider me at all?"

The truth of the matter is that probably they have considered you too much, and they have deliberately kept this change from you to spare you hurt.

Or, on the other hand, it could me that we as children have not realized how everything has changed, and how we, too, have altered our behaviors over time.

It is a normal part of the human condition to want a smooth ride through life, so any alteration to that way of life can be unsettling.

But it is in how we react to that alteration that determines our personal journey.

If we fight every step along the way, our path will be a weary and troublesome one.

We will lose the battle against unhealthy habits and addictions; we will lose contact with our family and friends as they change over time; we will become depressed about how unfair life is, and how it is treating us.

However, there is a better way – the way of acceptance.

When we see that an alteration is necessary or inevitable, we can embrace the change, and go on with our lives with more serenity.

When we accept that life is a journey and that to stay still is not an option, we are better able to face the alterations in our lives with tranquility.

Assurance

We often look for assurance in the wrong places.

We may seek the approval of others to assure us that we are worthwhile.

This can lead us to do things we genuinely don't want to, and then to feel resentful that others "made us" do something.

We may think that money or fame or some other external means of approval will give us the assurance that we seek.

Even if we succeed in these ways, the amount of money we can make is finite, and fame can bring its own problems. The chances are that there will be others who have more money than us, or greater notoriety.

Even if we do not seek to be the best or the greatest, we may still seek assurance of our value in the respect of others, in working hard, in doing good deeds.

Or, at the other extreme, in creating the most fear, doing the least we can to get by, or in cheating and lying.

Most of us, of course, do not show these extremes but are a collection of small parts of all these traits, on occasion both worthy and shameful, kind and cruel.

But really, what is the assurance that we seek?

I think it is the assurance that we are worth something.

It is in working out how to define what that "something" is that we often look to externals.

We seek to show ourselves that we are OK by reference to other people, or to physical ownership.

If I have 100 friends' names in my address book, then I must be a good person.

If I own an elegant house in a good neighborhood, then I must be a success.

If I have a healthy bank balance and a steady job, then I must be one of the achievers.

But that assurance that we are worthwhile is likely to be transitory because it is always based on things external to us that we cannot control.

We may try to control them, and even succeed some of the time, but in the long term we are powerless over all things external to us.

In the end, the only assurance we can rely depend on, is the assurance that we lived this life as well as we could – that we did the best we could where we were.

The only assurance we actually have is that each day is new.

Calm

Some people can keep calm amid a storm, whilst others seem to carry the storm with them; why is that?

There are many things that we cannot control, and so we don't get to choose if there are troubles around us, or if all our plans go smoothly.

But it seems to me that feeling calm is internal to us, and not directly related to what happens around us.

When one person is faced with a loss it may be the worse emotional thing that ever happened to them, and their feelings overwhelm them.

Another person dealing with the same kind of loss will mourn, and calmly deal with the incident and the things that have to be done.

These seem such extreme ends of the emotional spectrum that it is incomprehensible to one person why the other reacts in the way that they do.

Some of this difference can, I'm sure, be explained by genetics and by our upbringing, but we also need to take responsibility for what we can influence. We can't change the world, but we can change how we react to it.

There is a point where we need to deal with our emotions – with great joy, with intense sorry, with success and with failure.

But we do not need to let these emotions take us over if we have enough faith to carry on anyway.

We know that everything will change – our sorrow today will become joy in the future; our success today will be counterpointed by failure on another day.

It is possible to be always looking at the past, or always looking to the future, but if we live in the present moment, we can be calm even when an overwhelming emotion hits us.

If we hold on to the one truth that "this too shall pass", we can keep calm amid the storm.

If we can enjoy the moment of success, we can be calm knowing that we don't have to keep at this level forever.

When we take a moment to pause, breath, and realize what we can control and what we can't, we can truly live in the moment, and be calm.

Clock

It is not until we step away from our normal routine that we realize how much we are ruled by The Clock.

Not so much by time – which is a constant factor in our perception of how our lives work - but by that abstract notion of what the clock says, and how we should react to it.

Growing up in the South East of England, I for many years lived in a town that was on the zero meridian, and so on a short walk I could cross from the eastern to the western hemisphere.

At the turn of the 2000's, there was a lot of interest in this, and a number of markers were put up on the actual line of the meridian.

That showed both the way the clock works, and how we humans give it more meaning than it actually has.

If I stood on that line at the stroke of midnight, it would have been true that the New Year had started. But what if I were 300 miles west of that line?

Because of our conventions, my clock would have said midnight there at the same instant as it did on the meridian line, but midnight as defined by the sun and the stars would have been some 15 minutes later.

And would it matter?

We live most of our lives living, not by what our bodies, or the seasons, or the sun tells us, but by a Clock that tells us the Time.

And I suspect that this is inevitable for most of us – we have to go to work, and our employers expect us to be there by clock time, and nothing else. Or we have a plane to catch which will leave according to clock time.

But sometimes it is good to remember that the clock is an artifact, constructed by civilization, rather than being part of our human nature.

So it is good from time to time to step away from the constraint of the clock, and just be.

We may need to take ourselves away from the normal world to appreciate this fully.

Even sitting at home with no obvious time constraints, our minds can easily stray to watching the clock, and how long it is until we need to do the next thing, or how much time we are wasting sitting here.

It is often only when we are outside of our normal routine that the clock can take a back seat to our living in the now.

When we live in the moment, we are really aware of time as a living thing, rather than the artificial constraint of The Clock.

Keep

Does what we keep with us say a lot about whom we are?

At different times in my life, I have been surrounded by worldly goods and had have also had only things I could carry in a suitcase – and I can't say that keeping all that stuff around me was any better or any worse than living without it all.

But going from one to the other did start to show me how to judge what was truly important – what I truly needed to keep with me.

When we have a pleasant home, it is important that we keep it maintained well. It is important that we keep our bodies clean and that we have an appropriate wardrobe.

It is also enjoyable if we are able to keep with us mementos of the past, to remind us of good friends and good times.

Such things as pleasant pictures on the walls and pieces of art are also good to keep with us.

But none of this is vital. We do not need to keep any of them with us for our survival or our well-being.

Indeed, it can sometimes be that we spend so much of our time on these things they take over our whole lives.

Perhaps we strive to acquire more and more items to keep, and that striving becomes a goal in itself, rather than a means to an end.

Maybe we want to guard closely the things that we have, so keep others away in case they want to take anything from us.

Or, having achieved what we wanted, we spend excessive time maintaining it – all our time is spent in cleaning the house, or polishing the car, or in some other way compulsively trying to keep our treasure special.

But the other extreme can sometimes be as destructive.

If we do not seek to look after anything we have, we will succeed only in losing everything that we could have kept close to us.

Sometimes, what we choose to let go of says as much about us as what we choose to keep.

Because it is vital to remember that we are on a journey through life, and it is not so much what we choose to keep with us that counts, as what we experience along the way.

Shadow

Can something thrive if it is always in the shadows?

Many of us live with some sort of cloud over us, hiding us from the daylight of the spirit.

Maybe we have a dark secret, and our fear of it coming to light keeps us hidden in the shadows.

Perhaps we have an addiction that we truly cannot shake ourselves of, and this leads us to cower from the light of the spirit.

Or it may simple be that we don't think ourselves worthy of the spotlight, and so we shun the limelight for the darker places where we can be "safe".

Not that I think we all the time need to be out there and that all our lives are open to public scrutiny.

We all have a right to a degree of privacy; we all have a right to hold to ourselves our most sensitive thoughts and feelings, and only to share them with those we genuinely trust.

But for most of us hiding in the shadow only gives us a false sense of security.

We think because no one can see our secret, it is safe, and we can carry on as normal – whatever "normal" means.

But there are two serious flaws with living this way.

Firstly we may hide the truth from others, and even try to hide it from ourselves, but we will still know that the secret is there.

Even though we try to stay hidden in the shadows, there is no hiding place from ourselves.

There are no shadows in our minds or our souls, nowhere that we can truly hide those truths we would rather not face. They continue to grow and to eat away at our serenity, even as we try to ignore or reduce the significance of them.

But even if we were able to hide the truth from ourselves, our hiding in the shadow does not protect us from the things we are frightened of.

Others can see our shame – even if not the reason for it, the effect it has on us.

They can see us hiding in the shadows, even though we may feel safe there.

To live in the shadows is to live only half our life – to thrive we need the light of truth to shine on us.

Happened

What just happened?

It's intriguing that the facts about an event are different depending on who is experiencing them.

We all tend to see what happened from our own perspective, from our own particular point of view.

And how we see things can often change even for us, depending on our mood and our sense of self.

Just walking down the street, and meeting a stranger coming the other way – we know nothing about that stranger apart from what we see, and so we base our actions on their perceived intent.

Will they be friendly?

Are they a threat?

Will they ignore us, or try to engage us in a conversation?

Should we ignore them, or acknowledge their existence?

And then we walk past and have a certain feeling about what just happened; we were feeling that the person was a potential threat, say, and so we feel relief that this dangerous person walked by us without hurting us.

Whatever our experience, we can be pretty sure that the other person had a different recollection of what happened than we do.

For them, they may have been expecting us to be friendly, and are suddenly unsure why we were so cold and aloof.

Let us imagine that they had just lost their partner, and are subconsciously looking for some kind of human interaction.

The simple fact of our apparent aloofness may make them feel that what had just happened was a mean-spirited person, deliberately stubbing them.

Two people, two remarkably different perceptions about what had just happened.

And yet to an outside observer, nothing had happened – just two people walking along a street from opposite directions.

Even from something so mundane we can see totally different world views, and this is increased many times when the incident is considered "important".

That is why it is so difficult to be able to tell what just happened.

Team

As a youngster growing up in the south-east of England, I was often asked "what's your team"; everybody had a football team that they "belonged to" in some way.

At school, we were encouraged to join sports teams – even those of us with two left feet and no coordination got to be part of the team, even if we were a liability to the side we were on.

But there are other "teams" that also define us in some ways.

When we talk about our family unit, we are – hopefully - a team all pulling in the same direction.

The same is ideally true of our work-place where we all work for the good of the company. I know that our experience can be, and often is, different, but the "team player" is an ideal that companies strive for.

Being part of a team gives us an identity and provides us with a degree of security. It makes us feel we belong; that we have a common purpose and a common goal.

These are all the positives of being in a team, the things that build us up and encourage us.

But there is also a dark side to being in a team.

When, as a kid, I was asked what my team was, my answer was as likely to be met with hostility as with acceptance, if that answer was "wrong".

Rival fans of different clubs can engage in friendly banter – but this banter can all too often erupt into violence.

Team sports may teach us interpersonal skills, but that can also teach us to hate outsiders, and be distrustful of strangers.

When someone is part of a team, they can use this security to do things that otherwise they would be constrained from doing. It can lead to the best and the worst of human behaviors.

The answer - as in much of life - is in finding the balance between the extremes.

We should embrace the good that being in a team has to offer, but be wary of the fanaticism that they can also encourage.

Our teammates can help us or hinder us as we travel through life - but it is our journey.

Look

There is a book I go back to from time to time and re-read passages from it, and every time I do I seem to find new things in it.

And yet the words on the page have clearly not changed – what is going on here?

The difference here is between what I see and what I understand, because my understanding changes all the time.

I can look at a mathematical equation, and all I see are squiggles and symbols.

But a mathematician can look at those squiggles and symbols and see the underlying meaning, even the underlying beauty of the equation.

And when it is explained to me in terms I can understand, I too can vaguely begin to look past the symbols to what they represent – I may never be a mathematician, but I can sometimes see how it all fits together, and take pleasure in that.

And so it is with many things that we look at, and see differently.

We may not have a teacher taking us by the hand and leading us through a mathematical equation, but we do have life teaching us day by day how to live.

What once seemed a straightforward matter, I may look at again and recognize as being more complicated than I had imagined.

Where I had only seen confusion and muddle, I can now start to see the patterns and underlying symmetry.

Sometimes, we look at something once, and then feel that we know all it has to offer. We can stop looking, not only to the things in our life, but to the people too.

We may once have actually looked at our life partner, but now we merely know they are there, and we assume we know what they are thinking and feeling.

When we stop looking, we stop giving ourselves the opportunity to learn; we stagnate in the situation as it is, rather than continuing our journey.

That is why it is so vital to go on looking, and not to assume we already know the answers, or that we have found the solution.

There is always more to look at, and more to find out – life is a journey, not a destination.

Merit

To merit something is to deserve it, but honestly do any of us get what we deserve?

What did one person do to merit success, and another to find only failure?

There are those who will tell you that the answer is solely about hard work – and I must agree that what looks like "luck" is often a result of a lot of effort.

Many people we are told are an overnight success have actually spent many years of hard work to get to the place we now see them.

And yet, that is not the whole story.

If hard work were the only thing to merit success, and lack of it a sure route to failure, the world would be a lot different from how it is.

Many people work hard at what they do, and yet still do not seem to get the success that is merited.

Other people do seem to get on in this world without any effort – their success seems totally unmerited.

How then can we seriously discuss the merit of someone, when it seems so randomly accessed?

I think the answer is that all success is relative; that what merit should actually describe is a good life, rather than one that the world considers successful.

If someone struggles all their life and ends up with little worldly possessions, is it that they did not merit success, or is it that their success was in proportion to what their desire was?

The line that sticks with me is that we may not get what we want – but we do get what we need.

Maybe to live a life of worldly success is required of this person, and thus they have merited all they get.

For another, the merit is in the trying – not the succeeding – and so the fame and fortune will go to another.

But for all of us, the merit we should look for is in the doing the best we can, where we are.

To be successful in living a day at a time is indeed a success.

Variation

The fact that nothing stays the same is well-known.

In fact, everything changes all the time, and everything is subject to variation.

Often, it is not easy to recognize this fact.

We say that everybody from this country thinks this way, or that the people who vote this way all believe like this, or that all people of a certain color have the same attributes.

When we use this as a broad generalization that is unfortunate enough.

If we genuinely believe that this is the case, it can lead to the worst kind of human behavior.

And yet it is easy to see that variation is a natural part of life.

If we look at a tree, it seems that its leaves are all the same – all a uniform shape and color.

However, if we look closely, we can see that each one has slight variations.

Maybe these are caused by differing light levels or animals affecting them in individual ways, but whatever the cause, they are all different.

We also have only to look at our own children – they take certain traits from their parents, but are uniquely themselves. Even coming from the same gene pool and being raised in the same house with the same cultural influences, they still turn out differently from their parents and from their siblings.

It may be easy to clump a group of people together and ignore their variations, but to do so is to ignore a real truth about us as human beings.

We are none of us identical in what we think, believe or feel, any more than we are all identical in height, tone of skin, or hair color.

Just as we all have unique fingerprints, so we all have a unique set of things that make us truly us.

It is in exploring the variations that we find true enlightenment and true acceptance.

Path

I like the analogy of life as a journey; it has real meaning and shows us how to live our lives each day - and so the path we take is important.

Our path through life is always fascinating because unlike a manmade path, there is no map to show us where the road will take us, no GPS to guide us as we reach a turning place, and we do not get to go back and start again if we make a mistake.

But maybe that is the wrong way to look at it.

Because, on this path, there are many turnings, may times where we have to decide which way to turn.

In fact, there are many hundreds of these turning points each day – every moment we are alive we can decide to move in this direction or that.

In this way, our journey through life is more like walking through a forest than driving on an interstate.

There are many possible paths; none are obviously better than any other.

I may need to take what appears to you to be a wrong turning in order to find a particular piece of my truth, whilst you may need a totally different life experience.

We can all make poor decisions; go down a promising path, only to find it is a dead-end; suddenly realize that the path we are on is not taking us where we need to be, but are unsure how to find another one.

Sometimes, I have followed what I believed was the right path – made what seemed to be the only choices that were available to me, and still felt unsatisfied.

Often these feelings come from not recognizing that there are no guarantees in life and that there are other paths that we can follow – nothing is a straight forward as it may seem.

In the end, it is not so much about choosing the perfect path, but about learning from the path we are taking.

When we realize that we are going the wrong way, this is not a reason to beat ourselves up or consider we are hopelessly lost.

There was an old hippie saying "there is no such thing as a bad trip" - to the extent that we learn from our successes and from our mistakes that is true.

The tragedy is not in taking a mistaken path, but from not learning from it.

There is always a new path to take if we are willing to recognize that there is something to learn even from our wrong turnings.

Notice

There are so many things that we have to take notice of in our day-to-day lives.

Road signs, laws, conventions, what our bosses want from us – all these things we have to take note of just to get by day to day.

And, therefore, things that don't demand our attention often fade into the background.

This is only to be expected – there is only so much input we can consciously take in and process at any one time.

The things that we need for our physical or financial well-being obviously take precedence over those things that we may consider "nice to have".

We may even come to believe that these things we notice daily are the genuinely crucial things – that everything else is mere baggage to be left in the background.

But to think that way leads us into dangerous territory, because sometimes we may not notice when we lose something (or someone) essential to us.

We can be so caught up in the daily round of living that we forget to notice how our friends or partners are feeling.

If we become so involved in our business life that we don't notice our friends anymore, we may only attract around us people who demand our attention, not those who need our help too.

And if that happens, then whilst we may have a lot of people we know, we end up in sterile and empty relationships.

If we are so bound up in our daily routine that we miss out on the beauty around us, we may be providing for ourselves financially, but be losing ourselves spiritually.

Things like playing with our children and spending quality time with our loved ones take time away from the things we notice most.

Having quite times when we can meditate and calm our soul can seem irrelevant when there are all these other important things to do.

We should take notice of our jobs, our responsibilities, and our possessions – all of these are important.

But whilst we are noticing the important things, we must be careful not to overlook the vital ones.

Activity

Isn't it strange that some days our time is full of different activities, but we have little idea of what it is we have achieved when we get to evening.

Often this is because we forget that activity and achievement are different things.

Sometimes we are so busy with the activities that surround us that we forget to ask why we are doing them.

We do all have some activities that we need to undertake – it may be work commitments, or household jobs.

It may be that we have truly mundane, but essential activities to undertake – for example, looking after young children can mean a lot of repetitive tasks, but we would all agree that they are crucial to the healthy growth of the child.

Equally, sometimes our tasks demand the utmost concentration and focus.

A surgeon, for example, is always aware of how the activities they undertake in the operating theater are vital and complex.

But for most of us, most of the time, the activities we find ourselves doing are neither complex nor vital, however much we may try to convince ourselves otherwise.

It is intriguing to see that many of us list watching television, playing computer games and surfing the net as the activities that take up most of our leisure time.

Are we just here trying to fill up our time with activity? Do we use the constant activity as a substitute for real meaning in our lives?

This is the danger; that by being active all the time, we do not have the opportunity to be still.

For it is in stillness that we can come to see if our activities are moving us forward, or if they are just using up our precious time.

When we have a time out from our day-to-day life, we can evaluate our activity to see if it is meaningful and helps us along the path that we are taking.

Or, are we using activity instead of growth – are we confusing doing and achieving.

It is important to remember that it is not how busy we are that counts, but how that activity is used.

Imagination

Having an imagination is one of the great blessings of being human. It is also one of the curses.

Our imaginations can help us achieve extraordinary things because if we can imagine it, we can make it happen.

Most notable advances in life are the result of someone seeing how the world is, and imagining a better one.

Having imagined a better solution, or a better way of living, they have gone on to work at a way of achieving that goal, often working hard and long until their dream is fulfilled.

In seemingly lessor ways, we can all use our imagination for the better.

We may look at the area surrounding our house, and see in our imagining how it would look with different flowers and bushes.

Having thought about how it could look, we go and buy plants and seeds and dig up the old weeds we had there, ready for our new plants.

And we work at the gardening year after year, talking pleasure in our successes and learning from our failures, each year getting closer to the imagined "perfect" space.

But there is also a darker side to having an imagination.

Sometimes, when presented with a decision to make, or a task to be undertaken, we can only imagine the harmful outcomes that could happen.

Or we imagine that people are whispering about us behind our backs, or are plotting against us, when this is not true.

At these times, our imagination can keep us trapped. We are afraid to move on because of the imagined problems that might happen, and yet we can see right in the here and now that our lives are far from perfect.

This imagining stops us from even trying, or if we try, makes us timorous and scared of defeat.

When we find our imagination turning on us in this way, it can be hard to change – but change we must.

Because if it is possible to imagine an adverse outcome, so it is also possible to imagine a good one. Sometimes we need to exercise our will power explicitly to stop our imaginations running the show.

And we don't need to imagine the future at all; all we have is now, and the future is an illusion, created in our imagination.

Physical

We all live part of our lives in a physical world.

You will read much in these pages about the spiritual side of our lives, and how life is a journey.

And that is true, and a good counter to the continual portrayal of life as just a procession of possessions.

But life is also lived on the physical level. I can be as spiritual as anything, but if I am tired or dehydrated, I will not be able to think many spiritual thoughts.

In order to continue along the path that our life is leading us, we need to be able to keep our bodies working correctly, and that means spending some time attending to our physical needs.

There are some who would tell us that this is all we need do – that just to "keep the machinery running" is all that we should expect from our physical life.

And yet, in the physical I can find a lot that is spiritual.

Watching a sunset, for example, is both a physical and a spiritual experience.

The actual photons of light are coming towards me, and my brain is interpreting those patterns as a sunset.

My eyes are automatically adjusting their aperture to the changing light, just as my brain is processing the signals it receives.

And, at the same time, a part of me is experiencing that physical action and feeling it on a different level.

My physical heart may be continuing to beat its regular beat, but my spirit is singing and rejoicing at the sight.

So it is with other physical sensations and happenings.

We are not mere recording machines that note the physical and move on to the next sensation. Rather we are inner beings, whose life can be exalted by the physical around us.

We are spiritual beings in a physical body, and must make the most of the experiences the physical can give us.

Plenty

All of us have plenty.

In this world, many of us strive for money or success, but find that we truly cannot get "enough". There is never enough money to meet all our wants because our wants just go on expanding.

There is always something more that we could do with money, so if we look for success that way, we will always remain unfulfilled.

And I'm not just talking about buying things – even if we decided to give to charity, or set up a foundation, there will always be more that could be given; more needs that could be met.

But, whilst we will never have "enough", we can have plenty because there may be more, but we don't need it.

When we look at our needs, not our wants, we can get to a stage of having plenty.

Let's say that I live in a three bedroom house, and I want to get a bigger one.

Looking at it this way, I need to see if I can afford the price and the upkeep, and be discouraged because I am unable to afford that extra bedroom that I so desire.

And yet, looking at it from the perspective of need, my 3 rooms may well be plenty.

I have enough to meet the needs that I have – more than that, I have them and can enjoy them, my cup is full.

There may be times when what we have is not enough, when to strive for more is indeed the right thing to do.

If I am living in cramped conditions, and have the ability to improve my situation, I am not saying that my need is to be ignored.

But when we only look at what we don't have, we become discontent; our wants are always going to be bigger than what we have.

Instead, if we look at what we do have, we can often see that the truth is we have plenty.

I think in essence having plenty is as much a state of mind as a physical thing.

Happiness comes, not from getting what we want, but from recognizing that what we have is plenty.

Concern

The things that concern us are intensely individual.

Some people are concerned, for example, about their outward appearance, and always want to look the best they can, no matter if anyone can see them or not.

Others seem not to care about how they look, and can turn up at a formal occasion dressed in their oldest clothes and think nothing of it.

In our personal lives too, we see that different people have different concerns.

Some will be exceedingly involved with others, and want to help them at all costs, while others seem only to be interested in themselves.

But what should truly concern us?

It is easy for all of us to get caught up in the minutia of life – to see only the trees around us, and not the forest that we are walking through.

Our real concern should be in those things that promote our well-being and our journey through life.

It is reasonable to worry about what we wear, as long as that outward show is not all that we are concerned with.

It is OK not to worry about the clothes we wear, but if our lack of concern there spills over into other areas of looking after ourselves, we could be heading for trouble.

Helping others is a delightful and worthwhile way to spend our time, but we should not be so concerned with others' development that we fail to grow ourselves.

And we should look after our own needs, but also we need to be concerned that we do not hurt others and that we help them wherever we can.

In all of these things, it is not so much the action, or lack of action, that is important, but our motives.

Does this concern help or hinder us in our quest for a more fulfilling life?

What needs to concern us is not so much what we see in the here and now, but the effect this will have on us and our journey.

Our best concern is that we do the best we can, where we are.

Cerebration

We all like to celebrate.

A birthday, an anniversary, a new child – all of us see the need to mark the event with some form of recognition.

And in the public arena, we have commemorative times specifically set aside such as Thanksgiving and New Year; every country and culture have their national days to come together and celebrate.

And so it seems to many of us that it is these "big" things that can be celebrated – that a celebration needs to be undertaken only for the public or at least shared with others.

My feeling is that we should celebrate everything that is special.

It is true that we should celebrate the public holidays, and the anniversaries and high days in our calendar.

But we should also celebrate all of the good things in our lives, even the "smaller" things that are around us.

When a child is born that is a reason for celebration, as is their first step, their first tooth, and so on. But each day that they wake in the morning is a reason for celebration because we get to spend one more day with this magical bundle of growth.

A wedding anniversary is a good time to celebrate the marvelous things that have happened in a marriage, but each day can be a celebration of continuing love.

Moving into a new house often calls for a house-warming celebration; each day that the walls keep us safe and the roof keeps us dry is another day to celebrate having a home.

There will be times when there seems little to celebrate.

Times when things are tough at work, and we seem to have no time to ourselves, or when a tragedy strikes us or those we love, and it is hard to see the good, or even to believe that the cloud has a silver lining.

But even in times of struggle, there will always be something that we can celebrate – even just that we got through another day, another hour, another breath.

And when we look for reasons to celebrate, the gloom can lift for us, and our journey is just that bit lighter.

Not everything that happens to us is wonderful, but we can find the wonderful in everything that happens, and celebrate it.

Garden

A garden – or a yard as some call it – can be a blessing or a curse.

Sometimes, we can go all out to make our garden perfect, and get real enjoyment from the effort, no matter what results we get.

But at other times, that pursuit for perfection becomes more of a chore than an enjoyment – just one more thing that we have to achieve, or one more thing to fail at.

On the other hand, we may decide that we want to go low maintenance, and just have a space for sitting and entertaining.

Taken to an extreme, however, this just leads to an unkempt and untidy plot that we are ashamed to call our own.

In many ways, how we look after a garden is an analogy for how we look after the all of our lives.

When we consider that we have to excel, that we have to abide by some rule book that others have written, we can easily turn this into just another way to compare ourselves with others.

And when we compare we always loss out because we are not the other person – we are just uniquely us.

Or we can take no pride in ourselves at all, and just exist in whatever situation we find ourselves.

When we do this, we end up dispirited because there seems nothing good in our world.

The weeds and the garbage pile up around us, and we seem incapable of escaping from the pit that we have created.

But – like the person who enjoys their garden – there are other options.

We can try our best for perfection, but enjoy what we get anyway.

Maybe we want a better job, but in the meantime, we do the best at the one we have because it gives us self-esteem to do so.

We remember that we are uniquely us, and celebrate our own selves, and so do the things that bring us contentment and fulfillment, even if these are not what others "expect" of us.

A garden can be a refuge from the stress of life.

The stress of life can be reduced if we cultivate a garden in our soul.

Collaborate

Whilst no man is an island, genuinely to collaborate takes practice.

All of us are dependent on each other in lots of ways; I could not build my car from scratch, nor could I create all the roads that I want it to travel on.

And we also collaborate in order to get the basics done; we all agree to drive on the same side of the road and to follow – well or badly – the general rules of the highway.

In these things, we may not think of it as such, but we are collaborating together to get a thing achieved – all of us get to our destinations as safely as we can.

And when we choose not to collaborate with other road users, things go wrong.

"Accidents" happen, and people are killed, hurt, or at the very least, delayed.

And so it is with other, less public acts of collaboration.

When we work together and know that we go for a common purpose, we can achieve extraordinary things.

When we work with our friends or work colleagues to resolve difficulties and problems, we find that the collaborative effort produces results that we alone could not have imagined.

If we have a life partner, and we seek to work together in our relationship, that partnership can only prosper and grow.

And then, we can collaborate with God (or the universe or whatever we conceive to be a power greater than us).

When we try to run the whole show by ourselves – to exercise our entire will to solve a problem – we may partially succeed, but most of the time we will find that it is too much for our own unaided self.

It is then that we need to collaborate – to seek to do our part – but ONLY our part.

I cannot control the whole world.

I cannot change how others act or respond.

What I can do is my own part, and leave the results up to the Power that is greater than me.

When I collaborate with God's design for the world, I find that incredible things are possible.

United

There are many things that divide us, and as many that unit us.

Sometimes when I look at the political arena I despair – there seems to be only discord and extremism.

No one can do any good, for fear of being seen as evil; any good that people try to do is jumped upon as being the worse kind of deliberately harmful action.

And this fundamentalism can spill over into the personal arena too.

One person takes his cue from an extreme view and immediately alienates those with more moderate views.

The most base motives are ascribed to any action, to the extent that nothing good can be seen.

And yet even here there must be something that unites us.

We may violently disagree with something said, but also to ascribe evil motives to this action is the problem.

It is helpful, I find, to remember that the vast majority of us are just doing the best we can, where we are.

Someone may take the opposite view to you on a topic, but do so for a truly compassionate reason.

You may disagree with the conclusion, but still be united with the person in trying to find a solution to the problem.

More personally, it can be easy to think that the people close to us are willfully misunderstanding us.

What may be abundantly clear to me, may seem totally different when seen from your perspective – and neither of us need be wrong.

This is the thing that can genuinely unite us – that even when we don't see from the same angle, we can at least acknowledge the validity of the others view-point.

All of us are walking the road of destiny at our own pace, and from our own personal starting off point.

But we can be united in the journey – because the journey is all we have today.

Custom

Coming from one country and living in another, it is fascinating to see how customs are often so strong that they go unquestioned.

What may appear an unusual custom to me, others see as the only way that something can be done.

And seeing that, it makes me realize how I too had not realized how my way of doing something was just a custom.

In my country of origin, we stand with our hands by our sides for the National Anthem, whereas, in my adopted country, we stand and put our hand over our heart.

Neither of these customs is right or wrong, just different; and yet the one could be seen as disrespectful and the other as overly sentimental, depending on the custom in your native country.

There are customs in our private lives too that can come to seem just the way things are done.

Some of these customs are benign – watching the same program every day, or wearing the same clothes on a rotation could be considered to be boring, but it does nobody any harm.

Some customs, however, can be detrimental to our progress in life.

Where we are so set in our ways that the customs we have come to use are seen as fixed and inviolate, they can become something more than a habit that is hard to break.

We may use these customs to give us a sense of protection – to shield ourselves from the changes that are the normal part of day-to-day living.

But all too often these customs become a strait jacket that binds us into a form of action that may not be the best for us or those around us.

It can become the custom to assume the worse in every situation, and always to look for the bad.

This can lead us to alienate those around us to such an extent that only the bad happens.

Equally destructive is the opposite extreme, where we look at everything through rose-tinted spectacles and assume that everybody is our friend.

The outcome may be that we are hurt and taken advantage of by others, rather than being on the smooth path that we desired.

In this, it is always worth asking if the customary is also the best course of action.

Because just as a custom can grow up because it is useful, it can also outgrow its usefulness and become a burden.

False

It is often hard to believe that the things we hold so dear to our heart may be false.

We like to believe that we are correct in everything, that our views are the right views; that our way of doing things is the only right way.

When we have looked at the evidence, and believe that what we say is true; it is not likely that we willingly accept anything else as truth.

And yet, sometimes our most sacred beliefs turn out to be unfounded – does that mean that everything we do is open to being false?

Even in the realm of science, where facts are checked and reexamined all the time, often something that has been accepted for years is shown later to be inaccurate – does that mean that everything science says is false?

I think it is both simpler and more complex than that.

Whether it is a scientific theory, a way of acting, or an inner belief, it is only as true as our understanding.

To the extent that our understanding is less than perfect, our conclusions will be tainted with some falsehood.

The old scientific reasoning was not false as such, it was merely based on assumptions about how the world worked that turned out not to be true.

When we take a course of action believing it to be the right one, and it turns out badly, it was not necessarily our action that was wrong, rather our understanding of what would happen was incomplete, and, therefore, a false result occurred.

And when it comes to the realm of our inner beliefs, there can never be an observable false, or an obvious truth.

What we believe makes sense to us, in our inner being and is, therefore, valid to us.

It is only if we try to impose our own beliefs on others that problems occur.

Because although we may have an exceptionally deep understanding of our own spiritual growth, this will be decidedly different from the experience of another person.

We all live in our own interpretation of the same universe, and, therefore, all have a different understanding of that is true, and what is false.

State

So many things come to mind with the word "State".

There is the country state, the condition of a system, even one's own state of well-being.

But the analogy that jumps out at me is that a geographic state is much like a spiritual state.

When we travel to another state – be it another county in our country, or a totally different nation – we meet new customs and ways of behavior that seem foreign to us.

We may like these customs or not, but over time we get to accept them as a new normal, and bring them into our own way of acting.

So it is with our spiritual state of being.

We may find some new understanding or concept, and at first it is strange to us, we do not understand how it works – or even if it works.

But soon we find that this new thought pattern becomes part of us, and it is integrated into our own being.

Sometimes, however, the state we are in does not sit well with us.

We may like the people in our community well enough, but the jobs on offer are not a good match for our skills and interests.

Or the job market may be fantastic, but the living conditions are not conducive to our family growing the way we wish it to.

In these conditions, many of us will conclude that moving is the best solution – that getting a different job, a new home, a new life in a different state is the thing we are compelled to do.

It is the same with our spiritual state.

We may have found ourselves always believing the things we have been given, and not moved outside those areas.

In some cases, this will be suitable, but in others, we will come to understand that this spiritual state is too constricting or in other ways does not meet the needs of our journey through life.

It is then that we need the courage to pack our spiritual bags and move on – to discover what the truth is for us.

There is no guarantee that moving to another state will bring happiness, but to stay where we are will only bring us what we always have.

Eternal

In a bar I used to go to, there was a sign that said "if you give up drinking, smoking and sex you won't live longer – it will just feel like it".

I smiled at that – and still do actually – and, like many funny throw-away lines, it contains a grain of truth.

Because whilst none of us can truly know the eternal, we can experience a glimpse of it from time to time.

We are transient beings, living in an ever-changing and transient world - our bodies change and age and one day will eventually wear out.

We can never truly experience what it is not to be in this state of change, never quite feel what it is like to be eternal.

But sometimes we can start to get a small grasp on a corner of what it is to be unending.

We are all different, but for a lot of us, it can come at moments when we are in nature; not just in the countryside, but when we have the fleeting feeling that we are part of the natural world.

Sometimes, when I sit in meditation on a deserted beach, or kneel in prayer, in a quiet church building, it seems that I am both part of the world but also somehow above it all.

It is as if, for that moment, time is irrelevant, and I am part of the eternal flow of the universe.

In my belief, I am indeed part of the whole eternal universe, but for most of the time it is not easy to feel that.

There is so much of the now and of the things I need to do that it seems that time is an enemy, or at best a demanding boss that I have to try my hardest to please.

But in those moments of quiet I can begin to let go of my understanding of what needs to be accomplished today – of what I need to have achieved by the end of the day.

Instead, I have a feeling that I am part of the eternal.

What is that eternal something that I am part of?

I can only know briefly, and in part, because my mind is set in the finite world around me.

But I know it is there, and here, and forever.

Promise

We sometimes give promises lightly, without even realizing what we have said. At other times, we know full well the solemnity of the promises we are making.

Whichever sort of promise we make, we normally fully intend to carry it out – true, there are some among us who deliberately lie and cheat, but most of us – at least in the moment of making the promise – feel that we will fulfill it.

But then life happens.

We say we will meet a friend at 3pm, but are held up in traffic and don't make it on time.

We may not be able to keep our promise, but we can call our friend to let them know we are running late, or reschedule the meeting to another time.

Or we promise to repay a loan on a certain date, but find ourselves short of funds fully to pay the amount.

Here, we may tell our lender the problem, pay what we can and the remainder by installments, so as to meet our obligation, even if not at the time originally stated.

But then again, we may have broken a promise that we assuredly know cannot be fixed, in the way that a late appointment or an overdue bill can be.

Such promises are not just the vows we may say at baptisms and wedding – they can also be unspoken promises we give to our friends and neighbors.

If we fail to meet these promises, we cannot simply reschedule our meeting or our debt.

We cannot simply say sorry and then carry on as we were, but often neither can we make adequate amends for breaking the promise.

That does not make us sinful people, just fallible humans who fully intended to follow one path, but end up going in another direction.

What we can do is seriously consider in our innermost beings before making such a promise, and to be realistic about our ability to control time and circumstance; to know that we cannot foresee the future.

And to do our utmost to be as honorable as we can in all our dealings, whether they be social, financial or personal.

Because a promise once broken cannot be repaired.

Playfulness

There is much in the world that makes me sad, and much that hurts me and those I care for.

Does that mean that all should be doom and gloom – that it is so serious that being solemn is the order of the day?

Whilst there is much to be serious about, there is also much to enjoy in the world, and many good people with great intentions and positive attitudes.

Therefore, it is good at times to be playful – to enjoy what there is that is great about the world.

Being playful does not mean that we ignore the solemn; we show respect for the things that need respect, but that does not mean that every situation has to be sad.

When we stop trying to control all the things that are in the world, we can also let go of the need to be always on our guard.

Sometimes, we can just have fun!

Because a diet that does not include fun is a sad one indeed; when there is nothing playful about the day then it is indeed a miserable one.

Sometimes, we need actively to look for the playful.

Particularly when we have a lot of cares, and problems seem to weigh down on us, it can be that are all we see are these problems.

When we are worried about a situation, or a tragedy has befallen us, it can take an act of will to look beyond the current woes to better times.

Often in these situations, we can't believe that happier times will come at all, but maybe we can know that someday we will be able to see that day.

It is the knowledge that things will get better – that time can, indeed, make all things better – that can help us when our day seems too hard to bear.

Looking for the fun can seem hard, but it is an essential part of the recovery process – without the ability to be playful we are doomed to stay in the dark.

Life is a serious business; that is why we need to be playful.

Early

There is something magical about the early morning.

One of my childhood memories is of getting into the car for a vacation trip – we would always leave extremely early in the morning to avoid traffic.

The familiar then became unfamiliar; our house was being shut up and the car packed with more than it normally carried.

Out in the street it was unusually quiet and even smelled different than normal. And when we left it was with a real sense of adventure – of doing an unusual and somehow daring thing.

What is it about the early hours that make them so distinctive?

I think that it is actually about us and our perceptions.

There is a natural rhythm to our lives – as human creatures we are programmed to work during the day, and sleep at night, and both states are familiar to us.

The transition from sleeping to waking is one where we slowly become aware of our surroundings – where we come out of our own minds and into the world around us.

We are used to the transition, but when we change our habit, by getting up particularly early, for example, we suddenly become aware of that changed state in a new way.

Being up early means that we are outside of our norm, and then we see things in a different light – booth literally and figuratively.

And this is like any change in our daily routine – at first all we see is the strangeness.

When we are in a new job, or a new city, or a new relationship, it is like the early morning – we notice the differences from our past experiences, and how different things are.

But like the early morning fades into the normal day-to-day routine, so the strangeness of the new fades into familiarity, and we forget about how strange it was.

Perhaps though, like my recollection of early morning family vacation trips, we should hold onto the memory of the newness, to help us remember how remarkable it once felt.

Being early can give us a new perspective and outlook, and that should be savored.

Act

We all put on an act to some degree.

For most of us, the acts we play are based on expedience or fear – and sometimes both at once.

When we are with strangers, or working in a business capacity, we will tend to put on an act relevant to the situation.

We may work at a customer service desk, for example, and have to act interested in our clients' activities, even when we are dealing with issues of our own.

This can sometimes be a blessing, because as we act in this helpful and pleasant way we can be taken out of our own problems for a few moments.

In a business setting, we will try to act in a calm and commanding way, even when seething with uncertainty inside – and this brings us to the second reason for acting – fear.

Because we often fear that we are not "good enough" - not smart enough or talented enough; that we don't really know the answers, but will look stupid if we admit the fact.

This "not enough" feeling seems to be prevalent in even the most outwardly confident people.

These acts feed off of themselves – when I act confidently in a meeting, people respond to that by listening to me, thus making me feel more confident.

This is the good, and the bad – it can mean that action gets taken where it was needed, but it can also mean that we act out of a fear of failure – and fail anyway.

In a business setting, this is bad enough, but too many of us also bring this into our personal relationships.

We may act like we don't care for someone out of fear that we will be rejected.

But by this act we set ourselves up for rejection since the other person will be looking for reassurance that we care – and when they don't get it, they will further retreat from us.

So we need to be careful what acts we take part in.

There is a time for acting a character, but there is also a time to drop the act, and be ourselves.

Thankful

Sometimes things are going smoothly, we are physically well, have enough resources to do what we need to, and are happy with our role in life.

At these times, it is easy just to accept it all, and most of us will also find it easy to be thankful. We will enjoy the good times and be happy that we have so few worries.

However, these good times do not last forever; indeed to some they never seem to occur at all.

We or those we care for are ill, or we have bills to pay but not enough money to do so. We may be unhappy with our work, or the people we work with, but be unable to see a way out to a better job.

We may think to ourselves that we have nothing to be thankful for, and so we sink deeper into the mire of despondent thinking.

But even in these hard times there will be something to bring a ray of light into our dark world.

In our journey through life there will be good times and bad, and when we look for things to be thankful for, we will always find them.

When we do make the effort to look for gratitude, we take one more step – small and faltering though it may be – along the path of growth.

It may be that all we can be thankful for is "this too shall pass".

It can be a comfort to know that even in the hard times there will be something different, although we may not know what or when.

And we need to be thankful because the alternative is stagnation.

If we just accept where we are – good or bad – as being as far as we can go, we will never find growth.

If we accept the good things in life without being thankful for them, then the exact things we should be thankful for will come to seem pointless.

If we do not look for things to be thankful for in the hard times, the times will go on being hard because we do not see any release from our woes.

Being thankful means that we can look beyond the day-to-day worries, and move on with our lives in a positive way.

It is easy to be thankful when things go well; it is a sign of growth to be able to be thankful when things go badly.

Delight

To delight in something or someone is one of the immense treasures we can find in life.

It is more than just liking, more than just finding pleasure – it is a far more fundamental feeling, and one that can move us to our very soul.

Sometimes we do things out of a sense of duty, and that can bring us satisfaction in the knowledge that we have "done good", even if we have not particularly enjoyed it.

Sometimes we can find a great deal of pleasure in something, and thoroughly enjoy what we are doing, but find that it is not substantial, it does not bring us long-lasting joy.

It is the same with people – we know lots of people we can have fun with, and those with whom we share a common interest, but then there are some who we just delight in being near, whatever is happening.

For when we delight in doing something, we find pleasure in the mere activity itself – it is not done grudgingly or from a sense of duty.

Nor do we do something because we think we will get a reward for it, or in some way look good.

In particular, we often delight in doing things for those we truly love, simply because of the pleasure it will give them.

Because our delight in something is not necessarily related to the amount of effort exerted.

A single flower, collected for us a loved one, can bring us more delight than the most expensive bouquet of flowers purchased with guilt.

The simple act of listening to someone pour out their problems can bring us a feeling of delight that we are trusted, even if we are unable to offer practical assistance.

And those of us lucky enough to have found a vocation that we can truly delight in know the deep sense of contentment that comes from following our hearts desire.

Pleasure is good; doing one's duty is great; being kind to others is wonderful.

But finding delight in what we do and whom we are – that is the most precious prize.

Labor

The word "labor" for most people brings with it thoughts of toil and hard work – of manual labor, working with one's hands and using more muscle-power than brain-power.

And yet I also feel that labor is involved in less manual activity – even in what I am doing right now in writing here at my keyboard.

True there is little physical activity - my fingers press the keys, and my head moves slightly as I check the screen for what I have written.

Even when this is turned into a book, it will be edited on-line and printed by automated machinery – there is little in the way of human physical activity involved.

And yet I still think of what I do as labor – why is that?

In essence, I think that anything we do can be called labor – if we have to work for something in any way, there is labor involved.

It may be that labor is mental or physical, or a combination of both.

But whatever the actual activity, to labor brings with it the feeling of effort – of things that do not just happening, but of work being involved.

A road is not something that just happens – it takes a combination of labor from different sources.

There is the obvious labor of the people building the road – digging the foundations, laying the concrete, making good the surrounding area.

There is also the labor required in creating the materials needed, and in transporting them to the site.

But also, there is the labor of the road designer in calculating the best place to put the road, and the materials to use.

There is even labor by the planners that decided that a road is needed in that place, at this time.

In just the same way, the words on this page do not come of their own volition.

It takes a combination of thought, experience and action – of various types of labor - to get them here.

So I think we all labor to make what we want come to life, be it a field of corn, a road, or another book.

Blessed

We are all blessed with so much – although sometimes it is hard to believe it.

There have been times in my life where all I could see were my worries – there did not seem to be a spark of light anywhere that would help relieve the gloom.

I am sure most of us have had occasions like that – times when all seemed hopeless and pointless; and what is worse, there did not seem to be any possibility of change.

At these times, it is hard to remember that we are blessed, but even in the darkest of times, it is possible to find our blessings.

Because we are blessed, maybe not always by the thing right in front of us, but everything we do and every hurdle we overcome is a part of our journey.

I have sometimes had to remind myself that I can be blessed just by the fact that "this too shall pass".

It may be unfeeling and unhelpful to tell a person that is grieving a loss, or is ill or mentally exhausted that they are blessed.

Even if true, it can be a hard thing to hear at such times, and can make us even more depressed to think that others do not truly see our pain.

We need to know this individually - know in our heart of hearts that we are blessed, even at this moment of heartbreak.

I know from my own experience, and that of others who had confided in me, that even the darkest moments when looked back on can be seen to provide a blessing.

We may have had a painful lesson – but as long as we learned from it, the lesson was itself a blessing.

Or we may have lost someone dear to us, and can see no blessing in it – but the experience of knowing that person for the time that we did was the blessing, leaving us a lot further on our path than we were.

If we look at what we don't have, or what we have lost, we will always feel discouraged by life.

But if we look for the blessing we will find it, and this will speed us on our way, if not happily, at least content that the world truly is as it should be, right now.

Moral

There are those who will tell you that there is one, very strict, set of moral codes.

Those that hold to this belief normally also know that they, and they along, know the truth about people's motives and that we all fail to meet these standards.

At the other extreme, there are some people who hold that everything is relative and that no one should worry about what is moral – the only thing to be concerned about, is if we get caught or not.

Of course, most of us are somewhere in between the two poles here, but we often stand firm on a few moral areas that we see as unbreakable, and reject the idea that morals are just "not being caught out".

I think the majority of us would accept that not breaking the law is a moral thing to do, and yet how many of us have not occasionally (or often) broken the law by driving above the speed limit.

We think that telling the truth is the right and moral thing to do, and yet we find that a lie or a half-truth comes almost unbidden to our lips from time to time.

Those who are sure of what the moral thing is in every situation seriously scare me, as much as those who do not believe in any moral code frighten me.

I am not God.

I don't get to decide if what others do is moral or not.

But nor do I have a get out of jail free card – I am responsible for my actions; I am responsible for following my moral sense.

All of us have an inner story that tells us what is right and wrong – it is part of the human makeup.

But we all have a slightly different sense, and simply to reject out of hand every other moral view is the height of arrogance.

There may be moral guidance that cannot be changed, but it is not likely that any one of us will understand it all.

What we can do is to act in the most moral way we know how to, right here, right now.

And as we walk the road of life, we may pick up more morals – or have to lay some aside – as we find our way to our destination.

Despair

If there is one place in the world that we don't want to be, it's in despair.

Once we are there it seems as if there is no escape, no way out – that the walls of despair are closing in on us, and there is nothing to be done.

Often, the cause of despair is truly an unpleasant situation – when we have tried and been defeated, and lost all hope that there could be any better solution.

At times like these if is almost comforting to give in to despair – that may sound strange if it has never happened to you, but it is the experience of many of us that we almost welcome the total surrender that despair gives us.

Despair can be worn around us like a thick, black cloak that hides our shape – and that is what can make it seem welcoming.

Because, when we have been battered and bruised by life, when all our plans have failed, and all our hopes are gone – what then is there to do, but despair?

Strangely, t is often from that pit of despair that we can start to find our way into the light again.

Sometimes it seems to be necessary to go to the darkest places in our heart before we can turn again to the light.

We reach what is called rock bottom – we are defeated utterly and unconditionally, and we cannot go on.

And yet, we do go on.

We find somehow that even in that despair we can still put one foot in front of the other.

Even when we have to go on without hope, we still, somehow, manage to go on.

And slowly we come to see that rock bottom not as the end, but as another beginning.

Not the end of the story – just the conclusion of a chapter.

Despair is a place that none of us would want to go to.

But despair is often were we need to have been, to get to where we are going.

Spring

I have never really liked New Year resolutions – maybe because of my experience of them and the reasons we make them.

For me, spring is the time for resolution, when new life is coming to the land, and the promise that this brings.

Spring is when all things seem possible, when suddenly there are bright flowers appearing where there had been only barren soil.

Even the air is different – crisp and new, bright and clean, after the dark and dismal days of winter, and before the sultry and hot winds of summer roll in.

And the analogy with the rest of our lives is striking.

When there is spring in our hearts and souls it is as if nothing can stop us, and there are no limits to our growth.

We all know days when there is only a little light, and we only trudge along, trying to keep ourselves going one more day.

And there are days when the world is settled for a while – the summer of our days when there is warmth in knowing that we have achieved some goal or milestone.

But when it is spring in our souls we have only the promise of what may be ahead – and it is that promise that is the most exciting.

There are the endless possibilities that only the growth spurt of spring can give us – and the possibilities seem to stretch out in front of us just for the picking.

As we grow older in years, we can become wary of the new, of the unfamiliar.

We can forget the excitement of spring because of the heat of summer, the contentment of fall, or the chill certainty that is winter.

But, unlike the seasons which come and go by the turning of the earth, in our heart and soul we can extend the season of opportunity, and start growing at any time.

When it is spring in our hearts anything is possible; when there is spring in our soul we can resolve to make the journey a memorable one.

Country

Love of one's country is a glorious thing; it can also be a curse.

It is right and proper, it seems to me, to honor the country that gave us birth; to celebrate its victories and mourn its losses. Our country can be in this way an extension of our family – it gives us another tribe to relate to and belong to.

But therein can also lie the problem, when love for one's country turns into hatred for others.

It is a sad fact of the human condition that we can turn a positive such as love for our own country, into a negative where we turn that love into hate, and think that all other people are inferior to us.

In our modern world, we see the two faces only too clearly – the pride with which we look upon our countries successes, and acts of violence against others who are from a different culture.

And this human conflict on the world stage is mirrored in our own personal lives.

It is wonderful to celebrate our successes, and to take pride in what we do well. It is great to look after our physical and mental well-being, to be the best "us" there is, and to use our potential to the fullest extent that we can.

That self-respect and self-understanding are what we should be looking to improve each day on our journey through life, but sometimes we can take that positive and turn it around in a negative way.

We can begin to think that our own success is all that matters and that it is right to trample over other people to get it.

Sometimes our self-respect can turn into a lack of respect for others, when we think our unique talents are not just different, but superior to those that other people possess.

And, when we turn that self-love into hatred for other people, we truly begin to turn our best instincts to ruinous effect.

Our love of ourselves does not grow just because we hate other people – indeed, it seems only to diminish our self-respect, meaning that we need to go on hating for its own sake.

We are like the countries in the world – we can learn to respect each other, and even celebrate the differences between us, or we can go to war to impose our views on other people.

For we are all different from everyone else – we are all individual countries in an ocean of individuals.

Persuasion

Persuasion and force – are these two faces of the same coin, or are there fundamental differences between the two. There seems to me to be a lot of similarities, and a lot of differences.

When we are forced to do something, our own feelings are irrelevant, and it doesn't matter if we agree with the action or not, we just have to do it.

Similarly, when we force others to comply with our wishes, their own thoughts mean little to us at the time – no matter how "good" or "bad" our intentions, the fact is that we are imposing our will.

There is some of that in persuasion too – there is something about making someone want to do an action when they are reluctant.

But in persuasion, there is more of the element of being involved in the decision-making process; more of changing one's mine and doing something that we want to do, or at least are compliant in.

And here is where we can see that this applies to our inner life, as much as it does to relationships between people.

For example, we may want to do have achieved something, but if we try to force ourselves into it, we are often unwilling to go through with the action involved in completing it.

However, when we persuade ourselves that the outcome is worth the action involved, we can accomplish whatever we desire.

A good example in my life is that I always wanted to have written a book - but that was not enough to force me into the action of sitting at a computer and producing it.

It was when I could persuade myself that I could actually do this, and then take the actions required, that I got the job done – I was persuaded by action.

Sometimes, no matter how badly we want something, it is impossible for us to change our actions to achieve it.

This may be an addiction, a bad habit we want to break – or a good thing we want to achieve, an action that we want to undertake.

What we need to do is to stop trying to force ourselves into the action – our will is not sufficient to do so.

Instead we need to use all our powers of persuasion on ourselves, negotiate and use whatever tools we need to.

The great power of persuasion is that soon we will want to do what we used just to dream of having done.

Wise

The world seems to confuse being wise with having knowledge, but the two are not at all the same.

Simply having knowledge does not confer wisdom on a person – indeed it is a common experience that some of the most knowledgeable people are often the most unwise in certain areas of their lives.

That is not to say that having knowledge bars one from being wise, merely that knowledge by itself is not the total answer.

A book can teach us all about a subject, but to be wise on that subject takes more than just the words from the book.

We can read all the advice there is on being a loving partner; we can study leading texts and understand the dynamics of a relationship.

But unless we learn from experience how to give and take, and how genuinely to love another human being without knowing why, we will not keep that relationship alive.

Because being wise implies something more than knowing with our heads – it means knowing with our hearts and feeling with our souls.

The truly wise person knows when knowledge is needed, and when it is inadequate to the situation.

A wise person will use the knowledge they have, but in such a way that they are not simply following the rules, but truly understanding them.

It is in understanding that knowledge becomes wisdom, and sometimes wisdom actually transcends knowledge.

Knowledge is limiting in that it has boundaries – it can only go as far as the things we have heard and read and learned.

Wisdom is about taking that further step after knowledge has done what it can.

For the wise person will know the rules, and know when to break them – when the facts are irrelevant in the face of the human need in front of them.

To be truly wise is to know that you don't know – that all any of us can do is the best we can with what we have.

And sometimes, there is wisdom in admitting that we do not know the answer – that our knowledge has failed us.

Because wisdom comes from the heart, not from the head.

Conditioned

How we think, react, and everything about us can be because of how we were conditioned as we grew.

The people with the most extreme views often have them because they have been conditioned to think that way.

But even average people can react as they do not from rational thought, or emotional response, but just because they have been conditioned to think and act in that way.

When we see someone of another ethnicity, do we react differently than to one of our own family?

When we hear a particular type of music coming from a car, do we assume that we know all that we need to know about the person driving the vehicle?

When we listen to a politician of a particular political party speak, do we do so with a filter that this person is good (if they are from a party we approve of) or evil (if they are from another party)?

All of these and more are part of our subconscious conditioning, part of the defense mechanism we use to protect us from too much information.

Because the world without making assumptions would be extremely difficult to get through – each time we came to a situation, it would be new to us.

Imagine constantly being like a one year old, with everything new, nothing predefined as friendly or dangerous, every option being open.

In order to cope with the world we organize and categorize and filter – it is what humans do best, and it serves us well in allowing us to go on with our lives.

But when we allow that conditioned response to be our only response, we cut ourselves off from a world of opportunity.

If we are so stuck in our conditioning that we never look beyond it, we will never discover the marvelous things that are out there in the world.

If we always do the same thing we have done before, we will always get what we have got in the past.

But when we are able to break out of our conditioned response, we can embrace the new, and shape our own path according to the world as it is, rather than as we perceive that it should have been.

Once we break out of our conditioning, we can walk the road of our life free to enjoy the world as it truly is.

Example

Others are often held up to us as an example – sometimes good, sometimes bad.

It is easy to look at the work someone else did and see where they achieved more than we did, or less than we would have expected, and we can sometimes use these examples to improve ourselves.

But all too often we look up too much to our idols, and treat them as if they were without fault.

In fact all of us, without exception, have some faults, some areas where we could improve – indeed if we think otherwise about ourselves, we are in grave danger.

It is normal human nature to be pleased when we are held up as an example to others in a positive way. We are rightly happy that other people look to us as an example of what they could do, whether it is in our private life, or our business affairs.

It is also normal to wish to hide those things in our nature that are less than praise-worthy.

We may hide these "failing" so well that other people only see the achievements, and we may begin to believe that we truly are as good as our public picture shows.

But inside we will know the truth – whether we acknowledge it or not – that we, too, are fallible human beings.

If we look up to someone as if they have no faults, then we set ourselves up for disappointment. When something less than perfect comes to light about our hero, all of our foundation of respect can go in an instant.

If we are the person being put on the pedestal as perfect, it can become increasingly hard to maintain that facade, and the higher they raise us, the further we have to fall.

It is difficult to comprehend quite how hard it is to remain as the example for other people – it calls on a lot of strength of character to accept it, whilst remaining humble enough to admit our faults.

It is good to have an example in front of us – it is better to remember that this example only represents one part of the whole entity that is a real human being.

Judge

It is all too easy to judge other people; to be the prosecution, jury, judge and executioner.

Because we believe we know what other people are thinking; we can tell from how they act and what their expression is what is going on inside their heads.

Or we see what they are wearing, what type of car they drive, what sort of music they listen to – and that tells us all about the person and what they think and believe.

We make these judgments all the time, and we assume them to be more or less accurate.

And yet, when other people judge us, we feel unjustly accused.

We know how our own mind is working, and yet others have made judgments about us based on our appearance or other outside factors, and come to quite erroneous conclusions.

In fact, we rarely have enough information truly to judge anyone.

We may assume from a person's vehicle that they are rich, whereas it may be that this is the one luxury they allow themselves, and they are struggling to meet the payments each month.

Or because another person has an old beat up vehicle, we may assume that they are hardly able to make ends meet, whereas it could be that this is an old treasured car, one of the many in the person's collection.

Any judgment we make about another person is almost bound to be wrong, simply because we are not that person.

And when we do get to know someone, it is often apparent that our first judgment was incorrect – we may like someone we thought we would not, or find that we have a lot in common with someone we thought totally different from us.

However, in order to get along we need to make value judgments all the time about people.

Should I stop and ask this person for help? If they ask me, should I give help?

We are bound to make mistakes in our judgment from time to time – the important thing is to recognize that our first judgment is not going to be the whole truth.

We can rely on our judgment to an extent, but we need to remember that this judgment can, and should, be changed over time.

Acts

Does how a person act reflect their mood, or does it change it?

I'm sure we all know of times when we have felt below par, mentally drained or otherwise not our "normal" selves.

At these times, it can be hard not to act in a way that reflects the mood we are in, to be sullen or withdrawn, morose or lifeless.

In acting in this way, we only reinforce the unpleasant feelings we have, until it seems the world has lost all its color.

On the other hand, most of us have had the opposite experience too – when we feel hyper alert and genuinely appreciative of the world and all around us.

Then we tend to be smiling and outgoing, alert and bright: we feel that we can make the whole world happy just by the sheer radiance of our own happiness.

In these ways, our feelings impact on our actions, but how we act can also change our feelings.

There are times when our good mood seems inappropriate, and we stifle our actions to fit in with the rest of the world around us.

In so doing, we tend to find that our excitement is diminished, and will eventually go entirely, leaving us with a sense of loss.

Equally, when we feel that there is no point in going on, and nothing to be cheerful about, acting in a positive manner can somehow help to make our day seem better.

Our actions and our feelings are like a closed system, both affecting the other.

How we act in the world directly affects how we feel about the world, and how we feel about the world affects our actions.

It is, therefore, good to remember that, although we cannot always control our feelings, we do not need to act on them, and that taking proper action can help to improve our feelings.

I may not be able to think my way out of a bad mood, but I can act myself into a better one.

Only

There is a great mystery of human existence - that we are the only one like us, and yet we are all totally similar.

We are the only people to feel the way we do – and yet all of us feel the same way.

Only we have the experiences that we do – and yet these experiences are shared with millions of other people.

Maybe this is because our uniqueness comes not so much what happens to us, but how we react to those events.

Most of us will fall in love at least once in our lives – in that we share our common humanity

But for each of us it will be different, because we are the only ones with the exact set of feelings and perspectives, and the object of our love is also unique – clearly this relationship is different from all others.

That is why we can both relate to others, and be distant from them at the same time.

To the outside world our life will look much the same as another person's life, there isn't anything particularly different about the external trappings of the way we live.

But our internal world – the universe each of us creates as we grow and experience life – is unique to us.

This simple fact has a profound impact on how we respond to other people who interact with us.

Our partner, friend or fellow worker will have reactions that we could interpret as being the same as those we know inside us.

The same is true of strangers, and those we feel distrust for – we can assume we understand their motives because we know what ours would have been had we done that.

But only that person can truly know what they feel and what drives them.

Their life experiences may have taken them to a totally different understanding than ours since they are the only ones who experienced them.

When we understand this, and work together for a common goal, we become more that just only us – we can be no longer alone, but part of something greater than any one of us.

Miracles

Some say that the age of miracles has passed, others that everything is explainable and natural and that there is nothing that cannot be rationalized away.

But I believe that this is to miss the point about miracles, because a miracle is something that can only happen to one person at a time.

When a child is born, it is possible to say that this was a purely physical and explainable event – and from the point of view of biology that is clearly correct.

And yet, for a young couple to hold in their arms their own much wanted baby feels to them truly miraculous.

Are we to say that this feeling is incorrect?

When someone has been held in the grip of an addiction, even to think of becoming clean is something that can only be imagined.

When that same person follows a path of recovery and becomes clean and sober, a skeptic could say that they had at last come to their senses, and worked hard at recovering.

Whilst hard work is necessary for recovery, it is also true that this seemed impossible before and that now to be free from their addiction is a real miracle.

The true miracles are all around us, every day if we choose to find them.

The flower growing in a war zone, a bird singing their song when all around is destruction, the particular way the sun sets on a significant day in our lives – all these are explainable, but also miracles.

The truth of the matter is that even when we can understand the reasons for something that does not explain it away.

The miracle is not, perhaps, that a child is born, but that THIS child is born to THESE parents.

The miracle is not that another addict becomes clean, but that THIS human being found their own particular path to recovery.

We are all miracles in our own way – whether we are dirt poor or fabulously wealthy – whatever we do, or don't do for a living – we are all little miracles forming a part of the tremendous miracle that is the human race.

Every day we can be sure that miracles are all around us – all we need do is watch for them.

Attack

All of us from time to time can feel that we are under attack, be it physical, verbal or spiritual.

Sometimes this is real – people will attack us from time to time, this is just part of life.

But often our feeling of being under attack comes from our inner insecurity, rather than from a real threat.

Often, when we are in a position of relative privilege over others, our instincts to protect our position cause us to see as an attack anything that challenges that power.

It may be that others have had a rough time, and are now trying to improve themselves, but we interpret this as an attack on our standards, and react accordingly.

We may see anyone with a different opinion to ours, not as just another person trying to find the truth, but as a threat to us – we feel that our very existence is under attack.

From an outsider's perspective, it is sometimes difficult to understand the vehemence with which some views are expressed, and how other views are vilified and viewed with contempt.

It seems that hearing another person's views with respect – accepting that there may be more than one opinion on a matter – goes away completely in these forms of "discussion".

Instead, there is no exchange of views, only a louder and louder shouting of the set opinions of the person who feels under attack.

But in these things, we need to remember where the attack actually comes from.

Because there should be a difference between attacking someone's views, and attacking them as a person, or questioning their motives in having that view.

In effect, we take on the position that we can never be wrong – that we are infallible and what we think at this moment is the final answer.

Often, the attack we feel is actually an internal battle between our own sense of us as fallible human beings, and our desire to appear right.

Position

Have you ever been stopped by someone carrying out an opinion poll and asked your view on something?

What I find astounding is that all of us will come up with an answer to the question, even if, a second before, we would have had no position on the matter.

It is as if our minds are wired to need always to give an answer to a question, and so, when asked about on a certain matter, it comes up with a position to take.

This may be of little consequence in most cases, but sometimes this inner need to have a view can be actively harmful.

Sometime, we may take a position on the spur of the moment, and then our minds start to rationalize it.

We come up with any number of reasons why our position is correct, and why other views are at fault.

Actually, all this is ego based – it is us wanting to be shown to be right, even when we suspect, deep inside us, that we may be wrong.

In fact, it is often when the position we have taken has little real foundation that we feel the need to shore it up as best we can, rather than admit that we may have been wrong.

In order to keep ourselves protected from any suggestion of being wrong in our position, we can become overbearing, or overly insistent, or just downright rude.

And all because we once took a position on something, and are now too scared to re-think it.

There are remarkably few issues that are so cut and dried that there is only one right position, on most things there can be a number of views, all of them "right" in their own terms; and all of them "wrong" in some part of their argument.

When we take a position that the only way is our way, we close down any possibility of change or growth.

We can learn from everyone, and from every point of view – we do not need to agree with everything we hear, but we can at least respect the person saying it.

When we insist that there is only one position possible on a topic, we close down our world, and make it a smaller place.

Speculation

I honestly think that more harm is done by speculation as by outright lies and gossip.

In our news organizations, there is always much speculation about what may or may not happen – what policy is or is not going to be implemented.

Whilst some of this talking about what might happen is reasonable, it is often taken to extreme lengths and becomes a feeding frenzy, rather than a rational discussion.

But it is not just in that arena that speculation is rife; in our personal lives we can fall prey to damaging speculation too.

Of course, when making a decision to look at all the options, and to take into account what may happen in the future is a good thing.

We can even speculate reasonably that if X happened, then Y may be the outcome, but not if we did Z.

It is when the speculation becomes a thing in its own right that we can start to get into trouble.

When we are unable to settle on one thing because there are so many other things that we could speculate about, it becomes not a reasonable look into the future, but just another means of procrastination.

When we hear about the actions of someone else, and start to speculate on their motives, we can be in a very dangerous area.

Not only can we never fully know the motives of other people, we are more than likely to project our own feelings about that person and their actions.

If we already dislike them, we will assume their motives to be bad, and in that light the speculation can go off the scale.

Once we have "proved" through our speculation the bad motives of someone, all of their actions will be seen in this light, even the best of them.

Equally, if we have speculated about the motives of someone we like, we may give them too much leniency, and not call them on things that should be spoken about.

The real harm in speculation is when we try to use it to control the future, rather than accept that this moment is all we actually have.

Social

We are all social beings, even those of us that act in antisocial ways.

Some of us choose to live alone, and many of us that do are happy with the arrangement and do not crave more company.

But even then, we are still social beings, and we do seek out the company of like-minded people from time to time.

The honest fact is that human beings are a pack animal, most at home with our own tribe.

Back in prehistory it would most likely have been literally a tribe, but that connection changed over time into families, countries – even football teams and gangs that we can align ourselves to.

We not only belong in these small groups, we as a species do best when we cooperate; but we also act at our worst.

On one hand, we can use our social skills for the common good, and grow both as individuals, and as a community.

But we can also use these same skills to exclude people, to make them feel out of the group and not included.

This is the unpleasant side of our social nature – that as well as feeling that we belong, we can also feel that others do not belong – we can actively exclude people that we consider being "other".

Given our need to be part of a social unit, to be excluded is one of the worst things that can happen to us.

If we are not able to find a "tribe" to belong to, all too often we go to extremes to try to fit into any group that seems less hostile than the others.

This can lead to what we would define as "antisocial" behavior – but is actually just another aspect of the social need in all of us.

That is not to defend the behavior – merely to say that it is the result of a natural human need to belong being thwarted, and being turned into a destructive force.

We must accept our nature as social beings, but also accept that the results can be good and evil, positive and negative.

Our goal must be to work towards a situation where we use our social humanness for the good of all – because our real tribe is the whole human race.

Head

Head knowledge is a marvelous thing.

We need to learn and understand so many things in order to go about our daily lives. There seem to be so many facts and figures to learn, so many laws to understand, and so much of everything that is needed to be done.

But there is a different sort of knowledge too – one that is somehow separate from this head knowledge.

It is like looking at an old master painting.

We acknowledge the wonderful craft of the artist that created it, and we may wonder at the ingenuity of the modern owner to keep it intact and on display.

We might even think about the value of the masterpiece if it were to come onto the market and all the history there is behind the painting.

But all of that we do with our head, with our understanding of how paintings are created and the economics of the modern world.

And if that is all we see and understand, then there is nothing else to say – but often, there is more to understand - a lot more.

Not just more to learn – for there will always be that; we may seek to learn more about the technique of the artist, or the materials used, but that is still head knowledge.

What makes it a great work of art is something on a different level – it is the way it talks directly to us – to our soul and to our heart.

This is somehow apart from the artistry of the piece – more than the canvas and paint, and the practical techniques that any of us could learn to do, given enough time.

No, the thing that makes it great is how it affects us emotionally, how it moves us spiritually – a great work of art will transport us from the day-to-day to a different plane of existence.

This is not something we can learn from reading or studying – it is part of who we are.

Sometimes we understand a thing with our heads, but often, really to appreciate it, we need to use our hearts and soul.

Existing

The philosophers of old struggled with the question of existence, they asked "how do I know that I really exist?"

The modern-day speculative scientists seem to be coming to the same question, when they look at different measures of time and space, alternative dimensions, and a unified theory of everything.

And yet these speculations fall in the face of the human experience, where even to question our own existence seems far-fetched.

It is obvious that I am here – can I not feel the breath in my lungs as I inhale and exhale; am I not aware of the existence of the things around me; do I not feel love and hurt, joy and sadness?

To think other than that we are clearly here – that we truly exist – can seem like the wildest of fantasy.

But even so it is worth remembering that perspective is everything.

To the lone hunter-gather in the deepest jungle, the existence of New York with its millions of people would seem ludicrous – how could such a number of people exist without access to the trees and rivers and wildlife that surround our huntsmen?

Equally, to an inhabitant of uptown New York, the existence of people who are not surrounded by all the conveniences of modern life seems literally incredible.

One's own existence we may not question: that others are truly "other" - that they exist outside of our own consciousness of them – that seems to be the hardest thing for us to comprehend.

In that sense, things only seem to exist if we are observers of them – if they in some way impinge on our own lives.

And whilst that may seem a narrow and insular view, it also shows something fundamental about the nature of human beings.

Whilst we take our own existence for granted, we actually create our own universe inhabited solely by those that we come into contact with.

Alone, we only know that we exist – it takes the interaction of others for us to know that we are part of a larger whole.

Together we can be sure of our place in the world – that we truly exist, not just in our minds, but in the hearts of other people.

We know we exist because our existence is validated by those around us, just as we validate them.

Heavy

Many of us have a heavy load to carry – but all things are relative, aren't they?

There are those of us who have some form of physical difference from the "norm" - we may have lost the use of one of our senses, or a limb, or in some other way be defined as disabled.

We may have the burden of mental health issues, or be struggling to cope with a workload that is too heavy for us to bare.

Even those of us who may be blessed with good health, a steady job and loving family, can still find the burden too heavy from time to time, and then feel guilty that we are not happy.

Each of us has our own burden to carry – our own set of issues and concerns.

The real question is not if we have these burdens, but how we handle them – are they heavy, or do we carry the burden lightly.

I have known people who took the weight of their burden extremely seriously – people who appear to want to put everyone else down because no one has had it as hard as them.

Equally, I am blessed to have known people who have not looked at how heavy their burden was, but at how they could make the most of the opportunities they did have.

In the end, it seems that if a problem is heavy or not is as much – maybe even more – about our attitude than the issue itself.

One person with a sudden crises will say, this is too much for me, I cannot go on like this, whilst another will accept it as just another round in the journey of life, and seek still to have a happy and fulfilled existence.

One person faced with a loss will carry that weight for many years, seeking in this way to show how much the loss meant to them.

Others will cherish the memories of the past, but carry on with their lives so as to show how magnificent the experience was.

There is nothing to say which is right and which wrong; indeed, the very idea of right and wrong do not apply here because every person's experience is unique.

It is only in recognizing how different we all are that we are able to carry our own heavy load the best we can, one day at a time.

Tried

We have all tried many things in our lives – what is surprising is how often we keep on trying a thing, even though we know from experience what the result will be.

We often get into our heads a way of behavior that we believe we should aspire to, and try to live to that example.

Sometimes that can be a positive thing if what we aspire to is truly a good way of living.

We can try to live to a code of behavior that we recognize as being of the highest value, and so to strive is a worthwhile thing.

But if we fail to live up to that high standard – and, as fallible human beings we are likely to fall short from time to time – we may have set ourselves up for guilt and sadness.

If we have a high ideal and have tried to live up to it that in itself shows our worth; even if we fail, we are not failures.

However, at other times we may have tried some things that we could not class as high ideals.

We may want to find happiness, and try over and over to find it in the bottom of a bottle, or a handful of pills, or even in a doughnut.

And whilst we may find some happiness there, the joy soon dissipates, and we find ourselves just as unhappy and unfulfilled.

The problem is not that we tried it but that we keep on trying it, expecting a different outcome the next time.

Having tried something that only worked for a short time, why do we repeat that experiment over and over?

At heart, I believe it is because we don't actually learn the lesson that we should – these things may appear to help, but they do not solve any problems.

Having tried something that does not work, the wisest person will learn from that action, and move on to try something else.

None of us can expect never to make a mistake – the only way never to make a mistake is never to make anything – the flaw comes when we fail to learn from what we have tried.

The path we are on will have us try many ways, and even a dead-end can teach us something if we are willing to learn and grow.

Answers

I had a realization recently – it was that I always have to have an answer to every question I am asked.

I think this is a common trait – whilst I may be unique, at least I'm not the only one.

The interesting thing is to try to work out why we have this tendency – why do we feel that we have to answer every question.

There may be an element of control here – by providing an answer we are showing that we are somehow in control of our destinies; that we know what the future will bring.

It may also be that we are programmed to answer by the society that we live in; from our earliest school days we are taught that we have to have answers to everything that the teacher asks us – the kids that answer are well-regarded by the teachers, so long as the answers are right.

All through our formative years, people in authority ask us questions that they insist we must answer – we are asked where we have been, or what time we came home, or any number of things about our lives - and we have to answer.

Some of us learn, in early years, to lie, or at least to be as economical with the truth as we can – but we still answer, even if that answer is less than the truth.

There is also some feeling of self-worth in how we answer – to say "I don't know" is one of the hardest things for many of us – it can feel like an admission of failure to admit to not knowing.

And maybe we get here to the underlying motive behind my always needing to answer a question.

If I am in any way feeling less-than about myself, it may feel that I need to provide an answer, even where no answer is possible, to help lessen that feeling.

When I am unsure of my ground, it may feel safer to answer a question – even if to do so is meaningless – than simply to remain silent.

It can take more strength to refrain from answering, than to provide an answer where none is genuinely needed.

I need to remind myself that I am enough – and that sometimes the best answer is none at all.

Rest

It is a sign of weakness to need to rest?

There is much in our society that seems to point in that direction – in many work places we are expected to give 110%, and whilst we may smile at the logical impossibility of doing so, the ethos it promotes is a strange one.

I once worked in an office where a group of people were exalted for the amount of time they spent working.

It was the "macho" thing to do to be at one's desk from early morning until late in the evening, and the people themselves only extended that ethos by saying how many hours they put in.

When I moved into that team I was surprised to find I could complete all my tasks in a normal working day; it soon dawned on me that working these long hours was just what one did, regardless of the need.

Rest is important for our bodies – our minds become cluttered and do not function well if we do not get enough sleep, and we need "down time" away from constant activity. Indeed, every training regime for athletes include some time to rest, to allow the body to recuperate.

But just as we allow our bodies to relax, so we need to do the same in our mental and spiritual lives.

Our minds can be in a whirl, even when our body is at rest: for some of us, it seems impossible to turn off the incessant worrying and questioning that our heads take on.

It is, of course, part of human nature never fully to turn off, but at least for some time each day it is good consciously to rest our thinking, and allow ourselves some peace.

How often we hear that someone likes to watch mindless television at the end of the day; it gives us a different focus from our normal thoughts.

To be mindless – without conscious thought processing – gives our spirits time to rest from the constant buffeting of our own thinking.

Many of us need to take an active role in this mind-less start through meditation or simply by having some quiet time, where we do not need to concentrate on the things we are to do next.

And when our minds and souls rest in this way, something magical happens.

When we are set free from the mundane thoughts that occupy our heads, we can become more truly us – individual beings, not just a collection of actions.

Rest can give us the space to be the people we were meant to be, rather than just the sum of the things we do.

Easy

So many things seem too hard in our daily lives.

It may be that we have a new job to do, or a difficult task to undertake; perhaps just getting up in the morning seems too hard.

But sometimes, those exact things we thought seemed hardest, are really easy to accomplish.

The truth is that everything is easy if we know what we are doing, and are motivated to do it - both of those conditions are necessary.

When we start something new – be it a new task, or doing a familiar thing in a new way – at first we do not exactly understand what we are to do, and it takes time to be familiar with the activity.

But slowly over time the unfamiliar becomes ordinary, and we learn what to do and how to do it.

At that stage, we may think that it is now easy to accomplish the task at hand, but sometimes it is not; even though we know the how-to – we don't have any desire to do it.

Our lack of motivation means that even though we know what to do, we are finding it hard to do so.

We want the outcome, but are unwilling to go through the pain of completing the actions necessary for it to be accomplished.

This is a frustrating stage to be at – somewhere between unknowing and unwilling – and sometimes we have just to roll up our sleeves and get on with it.

Because what is easy, and what is hard, are relative concepts.

If I am willing to learn a new task, then I can accomplish it with comparative ease – but if I learn something without the willingness to accomplish it, than it will never seem easy.

So it is with many things – the ease comes with repetition, but repetition takes the willingness to do it even when we don't want to.

Everything is easy once our knowledge of what to do is matched with our willingness to do it.

Atmosphere

There are sometimes things that we can sense, without quite being aware of how – and one of them is the atmosphere of a place or a building.

Sometimes we can go into a space and know something about it inside of us, apparently without knowing facts about the place.

Some of this feeling of atmosphere comes, I am sure, from deep cultural instincts.

When we walk into a room, and everyone stops talking, we may say that there was a bad atmosphere, but actually, we are just attuned to how other people react, and are responding accordingly.

Equally, if I walk into a room and people smile and greet me, it is not necessarily an intangible "atmosphere" that I am picking up on, so much as the body language cues of those around me.

So when, for example, we go into a church or temple, we will bring with us our own conceptions of what such a building should feel like.

We may expect it to be calm and contemplative, and so that is what we go in looking for.

Or we may think that all religious feeling is misguided at best, and so enter the building expecting to find mambo-jumbo rhetoric and hostile people, and be extra guarded against the place.

But that does not explain all of the feeling of atmospherics that we have.

For example, I have my own set of conceptions of what a church "should" feel like.

But I have been in churches that have felt like they were just buildings, others that felt more like a market – but also others that filled me with a sense of awe and reverence.

I can probably find rationalizations for some of the feelings – maybe one spelled of candles which brought back a childhood memory, or another was noisy and brash, and it seemed to be about money.

But these are trivial cues - there is still an "other-ness" about some places that seem not at all connected with their physical presence.

After all the logic has been used up, it sometimes just comes down to being something in the atmosphere.

Messages

It seems part of the human condition that the messages we receive are totally different from the messages that are sent out.

How many times have we said something, only to find that our message has been misinterpreted?

It seems that whatever we say, someone, somewhere will – seemingly on purpose – misunderstand the message we are trying to convey.

I might try gently to tell someone the quotations they are using is wrong, and be accused of acting like God and wanting everyone to do things my way.

Or I may ask a question because I am unsure of the answer, but the message someone else gets is that I mistrust and disbelieve them.

From hearing the experiences of other people, I know that I am not unique in this regard – most of us have the same experiences over and over again.

How is it that our messages can be so mistaken from what we meant, and we can so often misunderstand the messages coming from other people?

The answer lies in the uniqueness of each of us and of our experiences and outlooks.

Whilst one person may have the experience of open questioning to be a positive thing, another may have only experienced it in a totally negative and destructive way.

Their experience of question asking may be that they were always used when the speaker knew the answer, and were merely trying to trip them up; they were being set up to fail.

Thus, the same piece of conversation may sound totally different from the perspective of the two people involved.

What is to be done?

Since we are unable to change other people, the only solution is to try to look at each message, not from our own perspective, but of the other person.

From what I know of this person, is it likely that they are deliberately trying to trick me?

Given my previous experience, is their reaction to what I said a real disagreement, or have they received a different message than the one I intended?

In the end, we can only be responsible for our own messages – we should strive to say what we mean and mean what we say, whilst accepting that what is sent and what is received are often remarkably different things.

Weakness

We have all been taught that we must always appear strong, and so, over time, we become to think that this is the only way to be.

Even if we are terrified of the way our life is going, we strive to maintain our outward display of strength because to admit our weakness seems too difficult to do.

There is a great deal that is good in this because sometimes we need just to carry on, regardless of how we feel about a situation. Often we find that when we battle on against our weakness, we win through anyway – and even if not, at least the effort in itself was worthwhile.

However, sometimes to be able to carry on, we need to acknowledge our weakness; to see the truth in a situation over which we have no power. Because to pretend strength when we are weak is to fool ourselves about the real situation.

Sometimes we are weaker than the situation, sometimes we truly cannot do it alone from our own willpower.

It is at times like these that pretending to ourselves that we do have the power to continue will only lead to pain and heartache. And this is not just about physical strength; it can also be about our spiritual or emotional weakness.

When a loved one has gone from our lives we can feel that we have no strength to carry on, and if we do not admit that weakness, it will build up inside us until we completely disintegrate.

When we face a fear, we can try to battle through it, but often that will only result in us being defeated by our own emotions: acknowledging that we are weak, and that along we cannot do this can give us the courage to carry on anyway.

It may seem that admitting our weaknesses is the way of the coward, but I would suggest that it takes real courage to admit that we are weak and in need of help.

That help may be practical, but more often in our lives it is the moral support of friends and family, or the spiritual support from a power greater than us.

When we pretend we are strong, we can snap in the gale, but if we admit our weakness and bend with the wind, we can outlive the storm.

We are all taught that we need to be strong, but sometimes our greatest strength comes in accepting our weakness.

Failure

I think we all like to look upon ourselves as successful – there are very few of us that like admitting we have failed.

And yet failure is an almost inevitable part of our lives as growing human beings.

I say "almost" because there is one way to ensure that we never fail, and that is never to try, but that way leads only to more discouragement and embitterment.

For most of us, we will often try new things, or to do old things in a new way, and it is from these experiences that we learn.

It is hardly likely, however, that all our efforts will succeed, and sometimes failures come along so regularly that we can start to think of ourselves as failures.

The truth is that we are never failures just because we fail – if we have failed it means that we tried, and are doing the best we can do.

If we do feel like failures, we are less likely to carry on and try again, and in not trying we do become failures – failures to be all that we should be.

Because it is in trying that we learn what works, and – just as importantly – what does not work.

We learn as much from our failure as we do from our success, and if we do not learn from our failures, we are bound to repeat them.

It is important to remember that this is a process – a journey – as we learn one new lesson, there are any number of other lessons springing up ready to be learned.

Failure can hurt – we may have put so much effort into this thing that to fail makes us ache inside.

It can be easy to think that this failure means that we will never succeed; that we can never reach our goal.

But the history of life shows us that it takes all the lessons, and all the failures, finally to reach a successful conclusion.

And more than that, each conclusion can lead to a new stage of our journey, a new place to carry on from.

Failure is a common experience – it is what we do having failed that defines us.

Pain

Pain comes in many forms – some we can see in others, and some we only know about from experience.

When we see someone wince as they stand up, or grunt as they lift a package, we can relate to that pain as we, ourselves have also felt that pain in similar circumstances.

When we hear about someone with a disease or injury, even if we have not suffered from that ailment we can probably still relate the pain to something in our own lives – we know similar pain, even if we have not felt that exact same problem.

But what about the things that we cannot "see" - the emotional or spiritual pain that is not normally manifest on our body – what of that type of pain?

We can often relate to that as well if we are aware of it, but the issue can come when we are not aware.

Often, when we have a pain that is not physical, we seek to hide it away from the gaze of others.

We may be hurt by the words of a loved one, but we keep the pain hidden under a smile and a careless reply.

There is a time and a place to show our pain – where an enemy has hurt us, showing our vulnerability can lead us open to more hurt.

But in most situations, there is nothing to lose and much to gain by showing our pain, because – strange as it may seem – we are not unique in our pain.

It is true that we are the only ones who feel the pain, but there are very few instances where others could not relate to our feelings.

Pain seems to be a necessary part of growth – each time we move to a new level of understanding, we leave something behind, and that loss if often painful.

Each time we open up to another human being we welcome in the natural humanity and warmth of companionship – but also open ourselves to the possibility of pain.

We may be tempted to avoid any likelihood of pain by keeping away from all situations which could hurt us, but if we do so, we also cut ourselves off from the possibility of joy.

Pain seems to be part of the process of living, and so it is to be at least accepted – if not welcomed – along with all the rest of the process.

Perceptive

Can you think of someone whom you feel is extremely perceptive?

I know that I've met such people – they seem to instinctively know what I am thinking, and what other people will do, leaving me wondering how they get to have such insights into people.

There are some people who are particularly gifted in this regard, and if we ever get the courage to ask the person how they often just shrug it off as being just what they see.

And therein lies the answer – because we can all become perceptive when we notice things that others disregard.

How does a mother know instantly when her child is in trouble?

It is not necessarily some inner sense that others do not have – it's that they actually notice all that is going on with their child, and use all their senses and thoughts to do so.

Where you or I might observe with our eyes, and then move on to another topic, she will instinctively see the action for something important and store it away for later use.

It can be the same with some deep friends and with our life partners – we can know them so well from years of contact that we notice something different at a particularly deep level.

We can seem to be acutely perceptive to our friend or partner, but actually what we are doing is paying attention.

And it seems to me that the greatest compliment we can give someone is to pay them attention.

When we do so, we get to see the real person behind the public persona; to see inside the mask that we all put up in our daily lives.

It is then that we truly get to know people, and allow them to get to know us on a deeper level.

What may seem to be a keenness of insight may actually be more about getting outside of our own universe, and genuinely observing other people as themselves, not merely as an extension of our own ego.

Maybe we are all capable of great perception.

Petty

There is an intriguing difference between what we think is of as important for us, and what seems petty in others.

The concerns we hear others talking about often seem of little consequence – we may think "how can they spend so much time thinking about that".

At the same time, we can spend our own resources on things which, whilst valuable to us, seem secondary to other people.

Why this disconnect?

Perhaps it is because we all create our own universe inside our heads, and so we all have our own view of how the world works.

To me, it is important to do this writing: to express myself this way is one more tool I use to help me on the road to a better, more productive life.

But doing so could well seem a petty concern to a homeless family starving in an isolated part of the world – their greatest concern is merely to get somewhere to sleep and something to eat.

That may seem an extreme example, but it is reflective of all of us, and of how we perceive what is essential.

That is not to say that everything everyone concerns themselves with is truly momentous, but rather that we need to consider the perspective of the individual, before judging the importance or pettiness of something.

There are many people who spend a lot of time on collecting, or in following a sport, or other activities that most of us would consider a hobby.

From an outside perspective, the amount of time and effort these people put into this relatively petty activity may seem ridiculous.

They may scour the country for the next object to add to their collection, filling every space in their home with these objects.

We, as outsiders, may feel this borders on obsession – indeed it can often cross over that imperceptible line and become an addiction.

But to the collector, everything else seems petty compared to the need to go on collecting because this is one thing that makes them feel genuinely worthwhile.

Thus, it is not petty to the collector as they must do this for their own self-worth, just as all of us do the things we find needful.

In the end, maybe everything is petty compared to the journey we are on through this life – that is the fundamental task we are engaged in.

Single

There is only one of you.

There is only one of me.

All of us are single individuals – and that is both the strength and weakness of us all.

As a race, humans gain immense strength from our "singleness", because from such vast variety comes all the good that we are capable of.

Humans have prospered and spread all over the globe because each of us have unique talents that other people do not – and so together we can achieve more than one single person working alone could do.

Our differences – our singularity – have helped us all become more able to live – some of us have provided ideas for technology changes; some have put those improvements to work; still others have used them to create resources for us all to enjoy.

So this singleness has been of immense benefit to the human race as a whole – we would not be where we are now if we were all the same.

The obverse of this singleness is that we can all feel intensely alone at times. This can have the effect of making us believe that no one else is important – that we are the center of the universe, and so what we want to happen, should happen.

But when we do that, the results can be some of the worse things that mankind can do to itself.

Wars and atrocities start when people believe themselves to be different – to be single and not connected to the rest of humanity.

On a more personal scale, we can take this singleness into ourselves, and hide from the world.

When we do this, our world contracts to the inside of our own heads – and that is a dangerous place to be.

So the singleness of each of us can be both a blessing and a curse – can make us a boon to humanity, or a drain on it.

Most of us, most of the time, try to keep a balance; to strive to accentuate the positives that we alone have.

But we need to remember that we are part of the human race, not single from it.

See

It is an intriguing facet of human life that we can each look at the same thing or situation, and yet see it differently.

All of us look at life from our own perspective – it is not just that we are all driven by our own ego; it is also a fact that we all have different experiences to draw from.

What we see and what we look at are two separate things, because what we see is a product not just of an external stimulus, but also of our own inner world.

This does not mean that what we – or other people – see is wrong, but it does give rise to confusion and miss-matched views of the world, and it is this misalignment that can cause problems.

You may have thought through an action, considered every angle, and come up with a reasonable approach to solving the issue.

What I may see is you doing something I don't understand, apparently without thought of the consequences, and so I may try to help you find the right solution.

In turn, you see someone trying to interfere with something that was going to work out just fine, but now is in danger because of my interference.

I may then get upset that my offer of help has been rudely rejected, and the feelings of rejection on both parts just continue to build.

And all of this is caused by our seeing the world only from what we know – only from our own limited view-point.

There is a delicate balance to be found here, and whilst we can never be perfect, we can strive to be better each day and on each occasion.

We are able to learn, but only if we are willing to accept that what we see may not be the whole truth.

There is always more to find out, always more than one way to view a topic, and when we realize that, we may be able to see things from different perspectives. When we are open to seeing things in new ways, this opens up for us the possibility of new horizons, and new interpretations – new ways of seeing.

Because once we can see things from another person's perspectives, our world view broadens and deepens, helping us as we travel along this journey through life.

Instant

More and more these days we seem to want instant solutions, instant results, and instant gratification.

If something does not go immediately as we would wish, we feel it is all wrong and that nothing can ever be right with us, unless we change where we are and do something new.

Change is a marvelous thing, but it's as well to remember that change often happens slowly, not instantly.

Any bad habit we want to change crept up on us slowly, bit by bit until it became a problem: it didn't happen instantly, and it won't disappear instantly either.

Any new thing we are trying will seem strange for a while – just like a new pair of shoes we need to grow used to the newness of it all, and not expect instantly to "get it".

We have to remember that life is a journey, and that means it moves on from one thing to the next, slowly over time.

When I travel, I sometimes wish I could have a machine that would instantly transport me from where I am to where I want to be, without all the inconvenience of moving over the Earth's surface.

The long car drives, the waiting in line for a flight, the seemingly endless train trip – all of that, it sometimes seems, takes the joy from the journey.

And yet some of my best moments have come unexpectedly during a journey to where I thought I was going.

The short stop for a coffee that turns into a wonderful exploration of a town I never knew existed; the stranger met in an airport departure lounge that has a captivating perspective to provide; the ever-changing scenery I drive from lowlands to hills to mountains and back again.

All of these wonders I would miss if I had a magical way of getting from A to B without any view of the land in between.

And in the same way in our life journey, if our goals were met in an instant, we would lose all of the joy of the journey, and the things we see along the way.

If we did reach what we think of as our destination instantly, then what? There is no final destination in life, and the journey will continue until it is over.

Instant gratification is just as instantly over – when we take time for the journey, we find that Joy is longer lasting.

Unwilling

When we are unwilling to do something – even when we know it is the right thing – the thing itself can seem to be extremely hard.

When we feel like this, it is worth looking past the action, to our feelings – why do we feel unwilling - is it reasonable, or fear based?

Often the unwillingness comes from fear; of other people and their reactions, of the outcome, of failure – or even of success.

Many of us live in a world that has been shaped by rejection in one form or another, and in that regard, the fear may appear "logical" inside our heads: why would we once again set ourselves up to be hurt?

But even in that fear, we can often work through it because it is the next right thing to be done – sometimes, we have to take an action, regardless of how others look at it.

Most often, when we complete a needful act that we were afraid to complete, we find that our fear was greater than any actual outcome.

We find a lot of self-respect in actually following through with a needful action when we are unwilling to do so. Anyone can do something that they want to do, to do it even if we do not wish to takes a particular kind of strength.

On the other hand, sometimes our unwillingness should be listened to.

If those around us are urging us on to actions that we feel are incorrect, or actively wrong, maybe we should attend to our unwillingness and take notice of our inner feelings.

It may be that our unwillingness is not a sign of lack of courage; instead it may be just the opposite – it may be that our inner soul is urging us to do something entirely different.

Often when we are with a group of people, there is a herd instinct that takes over, and the individual is swept along in the actions of the crowd. I am sure we have all known strong willed individuals, who carry us along with the strength of their rhetoric.

But still inside us there is a small voice of personal reason – a feeling that this is not the right thing to do, and an unwillingness to do it.

In these times, it is easy to put that feeling aside, and go with the crowd and follow along with others. If we listen to our unwillingness, however, we may see that this is a real, not a fear based, instinct.

Sometimes, we need to trust ourselves.

Self-control

The concept of "self-control" is an easy one to preach to other people, but sometimes it is hard to achieve in ourselves.

When we see someone drinking too much, taking unnecessary medication, or in any number of other ways harming themselves, we are tempted to think – or even say – just stop doing it!

Just put down the bottle, try living life without being sedated, or any other good advice, which would undoubtedly help improve their life.

All they need is a little self-control – if we can do it, why can't they?

And therein lies the dilemma, because almost all of us have ample self-control in some areas of our lives – but seem to lack it in others.

There seems, for most of us, to be things that we excel at but other areas where our self-control seems weak, or even non-existent.

We know we should stop this bad habit, but somehow cannot seem to do so for more than a few hours at a time.

Or we know that there is something we need to do, but somehow we always find ways of avoiding starting it.

There may be are some who genuinely do lack all such ability, but most of us are able to do the "right" thing, most of the time.

But in one area or another we seem totally unable to bring to bear the discipline that we show in other things we do.

Self-control is easy to show over things that don't trouble us – our real test comes when we find that our self-control is not enough to stop us continuing with something that we admit to being harmful.

At this point, we have two options: we can pretend that we do have self-control and that our actions are our own choice; that we actually want to carry on as we are.

Or we can do what seems impossible, and admit that our self-control is insufficient, and seek help.

That help may be practical, but more often it is spiritual or emotional.

An example from my life is when I eventually quit smoking after numerous attempts. It was not because I had suddenly found better self-control – it was because I admitted I could not do it alone, and sought out a support group of fellow quitters.

The simple act of acknowledging when our self-control is insufficient can lead us to a real understanding of ourselves, and help us to overcome what we could not do alone.

Mental

There are many physical things that can give us pleasure or can harm us, but one of the strongest influences on our welfare is our mental state.

Two people can have the same thing happen to them, good or bad, but the impact on them can be totally different, depending on how they deal with it mentally.

It is almost as if there is no good or bad that can be defined externally – much of it depends on the outlook of the person to whom it happens.

This is because our mental state affects what we expect, and how we look at outcomes.

When we are totally focused on one thing – our career, our collection of memorabilia, even such "good" things as looking after our home or our loved ones – this is all we have room for mentally.

So if anything else comes along that might, actually, be a better thing, we have no mental room to take it on board, and it slips away. We can sometimes be so preoccupied with our own issues that anything new is too much of a burden to us, and we would rather stay as we are than change.

Sometimes we can look at change as just one more thing that we have to cope with, one more problem to be solved.

In that mental state, it is not truly possible to see what is good because anything more we take on will just add to our mental load, and we fear that we will sink under the weight of it all.

And yet there is a solution.

We are not totally at the mercy of our mental state – we may not be able to think ourselves into a better mental state, but we can act ourselves there.

When it is all seeming too much, maybe we need to admit that, actually, it is too much right now, take a break, and spend time in things that help us grow, rather than keep us under.

This can often be achieved by taking an actively thankful viewpoint – even when we don't honestly mean it, just the act of giving thanks can help our mental world view.

By taking the time to develop a positive outlook – even when all seems pointless – we can work our way out of the negative spiral.

Our mental state can help us to see the positives in more things around us, which in turn improves our mental state – a virtuous circle that starts with one single act of thankfulness.

Speech

Speech is the main way we humans communicate, and so it is important to understand just what it means to us.

There are at least two elements to speech – the actual words spoken, and the feelings that come along with those words.

I'm sure we all know people who are accomplished speakers – they can carry an audience just by the tone of voice and the way of speaking, almost regardless of the message being delivered.

At the extreme, this can lead to both glorious and appalling things.

It can be used to rouse a nation to greater achievements, or to goad a crowd to atrocious violence, depending on the desires of the person with this speaking ability.

But then again, we probably all know of people who seem unable to get their point across to us in their speech.

They may have compelling and accurate information to impart, but somehow the way they say it leaves us unconvinced, if we even listen at all.

Yet we know that some of these people are genuinely caring and have only good at heart.

Why is it so difficult to ignore the one, or listen to the other?

At heart, it is because we do not only listen with our logical brains, but also with our feeling hearts.

We not only hear the words, but we feel the feelings, and sense the emotions.

Much as we would like to think of ourselves as rational beings, we are more likely to respond to a speech that reaches us on the level of emotions, than one simply based on logic.

This is both a strength and a weakness because the words alone are not always enough to transfer the meaning from one brain to another, so emotions help with this.

But it also leads us open to emotional manipulation where logically we would not take the position that we hear.

How we communicate is important – sometimes even more important than what it is we are communicating.

But how we, as an audience, react is more important – are we truly swayed by the argument, or have we let our emotions be manipulated?

It is essential to remember that our emotions are involved in hearing speech, so that we do not fall foul of the emotions of others.

Gate

I have an abiding picture in my mind of a country cottage, surrounded by a wooden fence, and an old swinging gate to enter the garden.

It is not a substantial gate – anyone could break in if they had a mind to – but it marks the place where the public space becomes a private area and is a link between them.

A gate can have this symbolism because it is an access from one place to another – a transitional area that we often don't actually notice.

But this symbol is more than just a physical location, and it can come to mean more than the strictly utilitarian.

A physical gate can be swinging open in the breeze, shut firmly, padlocked, even alarmed and covered with razor-wire.

And all of these may be appropriate – or not – in different circumstances.

A high security compound containing a store of gold probably does require a strong gate to protect it, whereas a cottage in a small friendly village would not need such strong fortifications.

To put the armored gate on the cottage would be unnecessary, and an open gate on the gold store would be asking for trouble.

And so it is with the non-physical gates that we have in our hearts and souls.

Some of us have become so afraid of hurt that we lock our gates tight against any intrusion.

We may have learned that to open ourselves up only leads to pain, and so we hide behind our locks and never let anyone in.

In that way we do, indeed, become safe – but it is the safety of the locked prison cell – no one can get in, but neither can we get out.

There are times when it is appropriate to keep the gate of our heart safely closed – but for most of the time, we gain most when we are like the cottage gate – open to the world and freely welcoming.

Because our hearts are not meant to be the sterile and safe environment of a high security compound.

We are designed to be part of life, to embrace it and welcome it in, and even if life sometimes hurts, it is the hurt of growth.

Since life is a journey, we must embrace all of it, good and bad, and learn to grow from both types of experience.

Because what is important is to change, and to do that, we need always to leave the gate to our heart ajar.

ABOUT THE AUTHOR

Derek Knight was born in London, UK and lived his early life in the South East of England.

After leaving school, Derek joined the finance industry, eventually becoming a Project Manager working in the City of London and Bristol in England, and Edinburgh, Scotland. Outside of his finance career, he has also been involved in a number of self-help groups.

After taking early retirement from this career, he lived for a few years on the East Coast of England, before moving across the Atlantic Ocean, to reside in St Louis, Missouri.

As well as these books of meditations, Derek has also published a number of short travel related e-books and is working on a number of other projects.

To contact the author, or for more information, send an email to:

CastALongShadow@Gmail.com

or connect on Facebook at:

https://www.facebook.com/CastALongShadow